# Praise for *Earth*.

"If there was ever a "bible" on handling and understanding the spiritual, physical, and mental processes of our lives, it has arrived. **Earth Life Challenges** brings us discernment through an Angelic Intelligence. True, brilliant, honest . . . This is awareness at your fingertips."

> **— Shirley Bolstok, author, poet, DNA "8" activations practitioner, medium, and Matrix Energetics practitioner**

"Very powerful insights on the hard questions of life and spirituality. The level of spirituality embodied in the channeling of the Collective is profound, and from a very high level, while being understandable and having many applications in our lives."

> **— David Barnett, healer/intuitive, and host of BlogTalkRadio show *Dave the Mystic***

"If you feel stuck in certain areas of your life, this book is an invaluable resource for getting 'unstuck.' A comprehensive guide to unraveling the many layers and subtleties of our vibrational world, healing past wounds and family traumas, or simply understanding how to clear unwanted energies—this book hits all the marks. I highly recommend!"

> **— Carrie Jolie Dale, author, *The 2 Choices***

"From the first pages, I was hooked. This book has a sense of sacredness and authenticity that touches our souls. I highly recommend. 5 stars!"

> **— Breda, Lightworker**

"Delightfully patient answers to our many human problems . . . Practical wisdom of the highest order. We are so blessed to have these words of Light and High Energy!"

**– Carla van Raay, speaker and author, *God's Callgirl* and *Healing From Abuse: A Practical Spiritual Guide***

"What a wonderful help and guidance! The answers offered are not "way up there" but down to Earth, so we really have a help in 3D until we can make the next step. Wonderful support on our often arduous way, navigating the waters at this time in history!"

**– Silvia, Lightworker**

"As an author and teacher in the Great Awakening, I find ***Earth Life Challenges*** greatly needed at this time. It gives you the tools and exercises to understand what is going on, not only with humanity but with Mother Earth, and helps you along the way to becoming your authentic self.

We highly recommend this book for anyone seeking guidance and answers to what exactly is happening on Earth at this time, and How and What can we do to help ourselves and others."

**– Rev Kari Chapman, author, channeler, and director, The Namaste Healing Center**

# Earth Life Challenges

## The Collective Speak on Dealing with Trauma and Life Changes

**Caroline Oceana Ryan**

Ascension Times Publishing

Text copyright © 2018 Caroline Oceana Ryan

Published by Ascension Times Publishing

ISBN-13: 978-0-9963138-3-4

Earth Life Challenges: The Collective Speak on Dealing with Trauma and Life Changes

Copyright © 2018 by Caroline Oceana Ryan

Book Three in The Fifth Dimensional Life Series

Cover design by Jen McCleary

For more information, write to: ascensiontimes@gmail.com.

www.CarolineOceanaRyan.com/

Published in the United States of America

**DISCLAIMER:** The information in this book, and all information written or channeled by Caroline Oceana Ryan in any manner or form, is not intended or implied to be a substitute for professional health or medical advice, diagnosis or treatment, or for professional financial advice. Health, financial and life results vary with each individual and no results are guaranteed. No writing or channeling from Caroline Oceana Ryan or the Collective is meant or intended to diagnose, treat, cure or prevent any disease or other life condition.

# Dedication

*To our Spirit teams of Angelic guardians, spirit guides, and higher self*

*To all of the Angelic legions and Archangels constantly answering our calls for help and encouragement*

*To those who paved the way into Ascendancy—the Ascended Masters, who by reaching enlightenment and developing their Lightbodies, encouraged all of us to do the same*

*And to every Lightworker walking the good Red Road to the higher dimensions while still in a human body. . .*

*My profound thanks, Love, and respect for all you are and all you do, at every moment.*

# Acknowledgments

My grateful thanks to early readers and reviewers of this book for their invaluable insights and support, and to my gifted graphic designer Jen McCleary.

Much thanks as well to all who are reading and supporting this **Fifth Dimensional Life** series, the **Ascension Manual** series, listening to the guided meditations, reading the weekly **Messages to Lightworkers**, and being an active part of **the Abundance Group**.

To all those joining together now to create the cooperatives, communities, experiences, and fifth dimensional consciousness of the New Earth: I offer my Love and complete appreciation.

I honor and support your path of Light, always.

# Contents

# Introduction

This third book in the Collective's **Fifth Dimensional Life** series addresses the huge issue of dealing with mental, emotional, and spiritual trauma, sudden shocks, unexpected life changes, and other crossroads moments.

It is not intended to be a psychological treatise, or a complete road map to solving every life challenge. As with all of the Collective's work, it is an expression of higher wisdom, Love, compassion, and pure Light, intended to encourage us in our Ascension journey. It is here to remind us we are never alone, even as we walk through the darkest night, and that our souls hold incalculable brilliance and wisdom.

It also expresses that when our soul seems to have run out of answers, some other beautiful higher beings will provide them, as we request or command that forth.

As with all of the Collective's books, the questions that start each chapter come from Lightworkers from all around the world, from all walks of life. Though they ask personal questions that relate to their own personal paths and life questions, all that they are experiencing is being felt by many millions around the world. All questions are answered not only with words of wisdom and encouragement, but with the energies to lift both questioner and readers out of the quagmire of feeling stuck and discouraged.

As with all I write or channel, I ask that you take only what resonates intuitively as being right for your path at this time, and leave the rest.

Thank you for your beautiful presence on the Earth at this time! We are fulfilling the vision we held, individually and collectively, before incarnating into the third dimension—for many of us, for the last time: assisting Earth and humanity in moving ever higher in vibration, until fifth dimensional life becomes an everyday reality on our planet.

May the Collective's words and higher energies bring higher Light, Love, wisdom, and encouragement to your path.

Namaste!

**1**

# On Discerning Whether Energies Are Your Own or Someone Else's

*How do I discern whether an energy coming into my awareness is really mine, or if it is coming from the purging of humanity's collective consciousness?*

*I am very empathic, and when these energies come in, I have trouble identifying whether they are something I need to look at, cleanse, and release, or whether it's energy coming from the collective unconscious.*

This is an excellent question, and one that is not asked often enough!

We would say that the two experiences are related. Everything you experience is a part of collective consciousness (including the *unconscious*). It would be impossible for any human being to experience anything, and not influence others with the vibration they are holding at that moment. Even a brand new experience would be added into the mix of what it is to be human now.

Yet you are correct that discernment is important. In fact, it is vital to your well-being.

So that when something moves into your energy field, or seems to be surrounding you, such as the atmosphere in a room, you can decide whether to hold and feel those energies, or to release them. When an energy comes into your awareness that feels heavy and dense to you, stop and *ask* if it is yours. Ask where it comes from.

Take a moment to ask yourself how you were feeling a moment ago. Has your energy dipped down, leaving you feeling a bit drained, weakened, or uncomfortable? You don't have to hold that vibration. Even a thought coming into your mind may not be yours. You can release whatever does not support your feeling good about life.

Of course there are times to experience anger, shock, grief, or feelings of detachment or sadness. Those are natural emotional responses to difficult moments in life. But it is important to understand when and why those feelings come in. And to ask yourself whether staying in those dense feelings for an extended period of time would benefit you.

A new energy flowing into your field is not always bad news. It is possible that an energy flowing into your presence is bringing something that has arrived specifically *for* you. Energies that feel positive and affirming, particularly if they light up your heart center, could be a message from your soul family, your Spirit team of guides, Angelic guardians, and higher self, or your twin flame.

These messages and energetic waves will feel uplifting and positive. They may come with a thought or a solution that lights up an issue that you have asked for wisdom on.

You could also be feeling the presence of a higher being you have called in as a guide, whether you have called upon them consciously or less consciously—in your sleep state, for example.

Or it might be the presence of a loved one who has passed on, and who is visiting etherically, and sending you encouragement or helpful guidance.

## Due to the powerful Light codes now coming into the Earth, that which you have been carrying unconsciously will often come to the surface to call your attention to it.

You may sometimes notice that you are feeling drained or less optimistic than you were a moment before, because you have taken on an energy that is not yours, and is not a support to you. Another possibility is that something has surfaced that you need to look at and resolve. Your subconscious holds a very deep well of experience, and due to the powerful Light codes now coming into the Earth, that which you have been carrying unconsciously will often come to the surface to call your attention to it. This may be something that needs to be healed or entirely released.

Nearly all human beings live in a cloud of thought, feeling, and reaction to experience, as well as expectations of future experiences. Beyond that, very few realize that the majority of these thoughts and feelings are not their own, but have been given to them by their immediate family and ancestral line, their past life and current life patterns, cultural programming, soul imprints, energy interferences, and other influences.

The all-important moment of discernment ("Is this really mine? Or is this coming from elsewhere? Do I really want to feel this now?") applies not only to that which may have come from the collective experience, but also to that which feels to have come from within you.

If something does not feel positive to you, think back to when that feeling began. You may be able to determine whether it came from something you heard in a news report, a song, a TV show, or a commercial that holds a low, dense frequency. Or perhaps a person came into the room who was extending their energy on an ego-mind level, broadcasting the density of stress, fear, anger, or sadness all around them.

These persons may even unconsciously pick up on your empathic healer abilities, which all Lightworkers possess (expressed in a multitude of ways). They may attach to you energetically in an unconscious plea to be healed, or to release the weight they are carrying.

These energy "sends" can also be telepathic messages sent to you from a loved one, or someone you interact with often. When you receive a feeling sense that someone is unhappy with you or has some issue that they are asking you to heal, immediately send a line of Light from your heart to theirs. This will keep you from being pulled into their vibration.

It is also a message of Love and forgiveness for all, and support for their path. It releases you from being subject to their dense energy broadcast.

## It is nearly impossible for you to experience something inwardly unless some part of your spirit resonates with it vibrationally.

You tap into the collective unconscious nearly all the time. Understanding it and lifting it to a higher resonance is part of why you came to the Earth again. This is a great, powerful stream of energy that you are a part of. It is almost impossible to avoid, though you can absolutely protect yourself from the denser aspects of it, including what some have called "psychic attacks," or just the influence of beliefs and expectations that do not serve your higher good. This is why so many use grounding exercises, and call in Divine Light as a protective field around them.

Except in times of globally announced emergency or disaster, you will probably not feel what the human collective are consciously experiencing as fully as you experience your own current life energy. Influencing this at all times are your past life and ancestral experiences, beliefs, and traumas. Dealing positively with these influences, drawing wisdom from them, and/or releasing them is another powerful reason why you chose to return at this time.

Be aware that it is nearly impossible for you to experience something inwardly unless some part of your spirit and psyche are resonating with it vibrationally, or are open to experiencing it. Form the clear intent and firm decision to rise above the denser energies you randomly experience throughout the day. You are capable of this.

You are experiencing certain feelings, influences, and ideas now because on some level, at some moment or layer of your experience at some time, you were open to doing so. There is something in that particular frequency that you resonate with.

This can get a bit tricky, because an empath picks up on so much. You may walk into a house or building that you did not realize was haunted with disincarnate spirits, lower entities, or other dense beings, and immediately begin to feel uncomfortable there, without knowing why. This is because you have keyed into presences that are there etherically. You may also have some deeply buried memory of having existed as a ghost yourself at one time, until some benevolent spirit led you back to the Light. Meanwhile, the friend you are with feels nothing, and can't understand why you prefer to wait for her outside.

In that moment, you are experiencing something you recognize as having been part of your own experience in some way, even if it's only a sensitivity to those energies or a desire to help that energy form or entity. You are also resisting being "colonized" by those energies.

We would say, that if you find yourself over and over again living in or spending time in places or situations or with people who carry a particular sort of energy that feels heavy or painful to you, some part of your spirit/psyche is wanting you to pay attention to that.

There are aspects of yourself that you have not noticed or given Light to in a while—aspects that expect those experiences, and may even feel trapped in them.

## It is vital to release all energies that inhabit your being that are not your true self.

Much of what you experience will come from other people. Understand that people who criticize you, make fun of you, belittle you in some way, or snap angrily or impatiently at you may well be playing the role of family members, caregivers, or teachers from your youth. You internalized the original experience, so that it became a part of your life experience.

In order to release those situations and step out of them without repeating them elsewhere, you will need to create boundaries—mental, emotional, etheric, and physical—that say No to those intentions and behaviors. And you will need to take decisive steps away from those who behave that way, showing the Universe and your own subconscious what you will and will not accept.

Humans invent new ways of experiencing energy every day, because you are in the transformative process of becoming Light Beings, evolving into that from a third dimensional body. Your body's vibration and cellular makeup (including your DNA) are remaking themselves to accommodate the higher Light now pouring into the planet, and to fulfill the new humanity's evolvement.

You are in the process of cleansing and releasing centuries of dense Earth life energies. In that process, it is vital to detach from and release all energies that inhabit your being that are not your true self.

You are a beautiful Being of Light who became human once again, to know Ascension again, and to anchor and celebrate humanity's and the Earth's path into fifth dimensional life. Part of that Ascension is becoming aware of what only a tiny minority of the human race have understood—that though you appear to be only one person, you carry with you the energies of thousands of other beings, due to your contact with them over hundreds of incarnations on this and/or other planets.

These presences can also include numerous entities and energy forms that seek out human beings as a physical base and an energy source. These can follow a person from one Earth life to the next, sapping their physical, mental, and emotional energies, and somewhat capping the extent to which they are able to evolve etherically.

The experiences and density of these beings, and their low consciousness, will contribute in a big way to the experiences of anyone they inhabit. Entities can have addictions, obsessions, various personality traits, fears, passions, and other attributes that their "host" mistakenly believes to be their own.

The other presences are often those of your ancestors, whose DNA you have inherited. This connection ensures that some aspect of their souls and their Earth lives remain with you, determining much of your life experience, until you release yourself from those frequencies.

Can you find freedom from these interferences? Including controlling programming and energy attachments? Yes, you can. Daily meditation that lifts your vibration to higher levels will assist in clearing much that is not your own. There are also numerous powerful shamans, energy healers, and energy workers on the planet now, in every culture, who are able to clear whatever you are carrying that is not your own, if you are not able to clear those energies on your own.

It is important to first accept that these energies, entities, and programs exist, and can inhabit nearly anyone, no matter how conscious and aware that person may be.

## Whether an energy comes from the collective unconscious or otherwise, if it is difficult for you, there is something there for you to heal or release.

In addition to any support you receive from an energy worker or healer, it is vital to begin each day realizing your own energies, your own presence and essence, before any other influence begins to invade, push, or influence your natural frequency.

We would begin each day, before rising, by giving thanks for the rest you have received, and calling back to you all parts of your consciousness from the various travels it has taken during the night.

Place your hand on your heart and declare: "I AM a sovereign being. I AM an expression of Creator God/Goddess. I AM rich with the Abundance that is Divine Love and Divine Light! Only that which is my true authentic self, connected to my soul and higher self, resides in my body and my energies. All else releases now, and does not return. And so it is!"

This centers you in a beautiful calm that nothing can permeate or disturb, unless you allow it to.

Declare to yourself often: "_____ [your first name], I know Who you are. You are not affected by the words or actions of others except in positive, affirming ways. Throughout today and every day, your individual vibration always stays true to your authentic self—your higher self. And so it is!"

Should an interfering energy try to enter your energy field, you are free to recognize such, having informed your Spirit team that you expect them to alert you very clearly any time your energies are being interfered with.

Declare: "This is my body and my energy field—only that which is of Divine Love and Divine Light affects or enters my energies, now and always!"

You are the sovereign commander of your life and energies. Anytime you feel yourself resonating with an energy that is not positive, health-building, peaceful, or empowering, ask your Spirit team of guides, Angels, and higher self to work on it with you, and to show you what it is you need to release.

We assure you, whether an energy comes from the collective unconscious or otherwise, if it is dense or difficult for you to carry, there is something there for you to heal or to release. It is a signal from your inner guidance that you are slightly off-course. Not in the sense that you are not heading into the experiences you dream of, for you still are, if you will celebrate and allow them. But in the sense that you have forgotten your higher self for a moment, and are living in the ego-mind, responding or reacting to something or someone that does not resonate as good and positive to you.

These reactions might well be coming from an entity, ancestor or other family influence, or a buried memory of a past life or current life trauma from deep within your consciousness. It is calling your attention to it.

Sometimes it helps to look at a feeling of anger, annoyance, or sadness, and say: "Where did you come from? What is your message for me? If you are not mine, I release you, and dissolve all contracts between us and whoever sent you, in all time-space. If you are mine to be healed, come forward now, and be restored to wholeness in the power of Divine Light."

Becoming aware of what energies are affecting you and why, is a complex process at times. But you are fully capable of doing so, and of winning your way back to wholeness, to the full authenticity, beauty, and Joy of your higher self—your true self—waiting to be rediscovered and celebrated again, after spending so long hidden, yet never lost.

## Grounding and Cleansing Exercise

Sit or lie quietly, breathing in deeply through the nose with mouth closed, staying with that breath for a moment, then releasing the breath through an open mouth, making a "ha" sound.

Continue breathing deeply in this way, releasing all thoughts. Envision all your supporters around you—your Spirit team of guides, Angelic guardians, and higher self, your twin flame, your soul family. All are sending you higher Light to sustain, encourage, and inspire you throughout your day.

See a stream of brilliant silver and golden Divine Light pouring down from Alcyone, the Great Central Sun. This stream of higher Light pours down through your entire body, filling your crown chakra with higher energies, as it fills every other chakra and energy center in your body and energy field.

It then continues down through you and into the Earth, where it streams down into Inner Earth. There it meets with the Great Crystals of Inner Earth, who receive this Light joyfully and magnify it all the further.

They send this Light throughout the crystalline energy grid that runs throughout the planet in a pattern of sacred geometry. That Light then runs back up through the Earth, through the Great Crystals, and back up through your body, filling your heart with an astounding, brilliant Light.

It then continues back up to the Great Central Sun, so that the higher energies of Divine Light and Love are flowing through you freely and fully, as you are grounded with Mother Earth.

Now call in St Germain or another Ascended Master—anyone you feel connected to—as well as Archangel Michael, who is a master of Divine Protection in this Universe.

See them putting a bubble of violet transforming Light, a bubble of protection, all around you, extending about 15 to 20 feet out from your body.

Then call in Mother Mary or Quan Yin (they are both manifestations of the same soul) or another loving Ascended Master, and see them putting a bubble of heart-based, healing green Light all around you, extending out about five feet away from your body.

Now call to the presence of your higher self, and ask him or her to step into your entire being. As they do so, they are also moving into all of your energy bodies (physical, mental, emotional, etheric).

Their beautiful presence now fills your aura with a third layer of protective healing golden Light, extending out even further the others.

These Divine Light fields now act to engage your energies in ways that are positive and aligned with your higher good. You may have images of things that have bothered you in the past—worry thoughts, sadness, your own and others' judgments and criticisms, mishaps, daily stresses—all bouncing off of these protective layers and being sent into the Light of the higher realms.

Know that energetic interferences of any kind wishing to enter your energy field, whether based in the ego-mind or other forms of density, are null and void now. These Light boundaries refuse them entry, as you continue to use this exercise daily.

# 2

# On Dealing with Intergenerational and Developmental Trauma

*I have been following a free healing trauma online program, and it has confirmed what I have been increasingly aware of, that early childhood trauma (and adult trauma) damages and impairs the normal functioning of the brain and nervous system.*

*This in turn diminishes our ability to have healthy relationships, to work effectively—to do almost anything effectively.*

*I now see that there are some subtle, invisible reasons why I am struggling to regain my stability after losing almost everything due to the 2017 northern California fires. That event took my residence, after which I lost my car and my savings, among other things that have occurred in the past year.*

*I've also lost my ability to continue my life work (massage therapy) due to changes in California massage certification requirements, my injuries from seeing thousands of clients over three decades, and other issues. All of this results in my being homeless at age 61.*

*These outer material challenges are exacerbated by my childhood trauma, which causes another set of complications that limit my ability to pick myself up and move on.*

*I was born to a well-intentioned woman who later in life was clinically diagnosed as paranoid schizophrenic. She was untreated during my childhood, so that while in the womb, I was already getting hit with fear, nervousness, and other energies that imprinted into my forming body, mind, and emotions.*

*My father was a very violent man. I witnessed him doing horrendous things to my mother, including attempting to strangle her when I was five. My horrified expression caused him to release her, and she lived. He was imprisoned for attempted murder.*

*I was also laughed at and picked on hugely in elementary and high school for being different, as we were poor and wore clothing that stood out. This also traumatized me, and I have struggled with low self-esteem my whole life. I have gotten some healing, but it's been a long, hard road, and I'm still not whole.*

*The online trauma summit has shown me how severe the effects of trauma are, dysregulating the nervous system and brain functions, unbalancing hormones and chemicals in the body. Trauma of any kind creates a domino effect—one problem causes problems in other areas, such as relationships, work, and everything else.*

*I myself have serious impairments—"emotional dysregulation," "de-personalization," and "de-*

*realization." I have an impairment regarding what is called "agency"—the ability to feel you can effect change, or the persistent feeling that you are outside of your body. I am glad to learn of them, however it's a little shocking. It makes me feel a little more despairing, as they are so serious, and I cannot afford the interventions these experts recommend.*

*This is quite complex and very challenging, because the physiological effects happen without one even knowing about it, which then creates difficult problems.*

*There are so many people affected by trauma these days. Intergenerational trauma is passed on to children from adults in the household who were themselves traumatized. Almost all of humanity are adversely affected and impaired by trauma, and don't even know it.*

*Think of all the wars, and the adults affected by that, as well as their children and grandchildren. All the minority groups—black and indigenous peoples, Jews, etc.—who have been severely traumatized by racism and genocide. Other forms of trauma include terrorist attacks, bombings, school shootings, etc.*

*I think there is also a lot of trauma generated in the new age community just in hearing about the ET warring races, and the mind control exerted over humanity by the reptilians. Trauma is so widespread as to be ubiquitous.*

*I have also learned that my recent traumatic experiences have triggered the prior trauma.*

*I am hoping there is an easier and quicker way to heal, other than utilizing clinical methods, as wonderful as they are now, with somatic and body-centered practices—far superior to the old cognitive therapeutic methods. We are in a new time now, with new energies.*

*We all have so much to take care of daily. Can we find a way to utilize the help of our spiritual allies?*

*Besides sitting down with our Spirit team daily asking for help, which is of course imperative.*

We are very pleased to have the chance to address these experiences.

We will speak first of what the unborn child inherits or is subject to, simply by "being there."

Trauma can indeed be passed down to a child in the womb, chemically and etherically, and via the DNA of the family line. This happens before the child has had a chance to exert their individuality, and to develop their own viewpoints or beliefs about life. They may intuitively feel the benevolence of the Universe, or their inherent right to their own sovereignty. On a higher level, they also know the power of their own soul to gain wisdom from every experience, while releasing any pain from it.

But their developing human mind, body, and emotions are now in a far smaller space that feels very separate from all of that empowerment.

As they receive the energies and biochemical results of trauma, illness, or any form of imbalance, their outlook on life is naturally influenced by these. You are correct that the child's entire human essence is affected. It also powerfully affects their ability to not only process everyday experiences, but to integrate them positively into the whole of their life.

Many do not have that ability to integrate positively. And you are correct in stating, behind the words you have chosen, that this does not feel right or fair. It would not feel right or fair, because it is the reflection of an entire planet in a state of imbalance, rather than in a state of normalcy. Earth life has for eons lacked the kind of easygoing, positive energetic flow and balance that the higher realms are known for.

**You came to experience this for the sake of anchoring exactly those forms of Light data that only you could anchor, in exactly the situations you describe.**

Once in a human body, you did not have the ability to fully integrate your mind and emotions with the imbalances you describe. And almost no one is born with the ability to see why these experiences are necessary, let alone that they might serve some good and positive purpose one day.

Your spirit was formed in the higher realms of pure Light—your life as a healer and caregiver are a testament to such. And so you came into a fragile Earth body, and faced very real, very tangible physical, mental, emotional, and spiritual imbalances, leaving you confused and isolated.

That is understandable. Yet you did not come to experience illness or violence or all of the various physical, mental, emotional setbacks you have experienced as a trauma survivor, to integrate them automatically and not be bothered by them.

You came to work with these energies. You came to notice and feel firsthand the strange and painful disparity between life in the higher planes, and life in the lower depths of this physical Earth life.

You experienced this not for the sake of living an impaired Earth life, but for the sake of anchoring exactly those forms of Light data that only you could anchor, in exactly the situations you describe here.

This is your true life purpose, dear one, as it relates to your physical Earth life. Most assuredly, the physical therapy you have offered thousands has been invaluable, and much-needed and appreciated. But it is not the fullness of why you came into this particular Earth life.

You came in part to anchor Light and the energies of the higher realms into those persons and their physical, emotional, and energetic selves. But only as a "sideline" to your true work of anchoring the kinds of energies that transform a violent, chaotic planet into a fully realized Ascending one. *That* is why you came.

Most assuredly, you could have come to Earth to live a peaceful and quiet life, surrounded by those who always loved you, protected you, appreciated you, and saw you fully for the beautiful Angelic being, and healing and empowering presence that you are.

Yet you would not have come in to what is both the most complex and also the most increasingly Light-filled era on Earth's timeline, just to have a nice time. You knew there is much to be done now. You would not have felt interested in an easy life, would not have understood the purpose and higher motive behind it, and would not have valued it.

For you have had easygoing Earth lives, in which most if not all of your desires were answered. Then you returned to the higher planes, looked back onto the far denser Earth plane that you had just left, and concluded several things.

For one, you saw that there was far more for you to learn, far more growth to be had on a soul level than an easygoing Earth life could ever provide. The challenges provided by the traumatic situations you describe—domestic abuse, war, starvation—are great and terrifying to those living them. Yet on a higher level, they open the door to even greater growth and expansion, however unthinkable any of that appears at the time.

**If you could see the brilliance of your Light, the power and beauty of your soul and all it has birthed—your true form—you would never again doubt your supremacy.**

For another, there is so much suffering in the world, that to return to a life that was less traumatic would not have assisted you in your work of healing and lifting up the lower Earth vibrations that have continued that trauma, one generation after another.

You experienced the depths of your mother's and father's mental and emotional illness, and the dark energies that lived in your father's body and mind and propelled him to do terrible things, not because you "slipped up" when devising your blueprint for this life, but because you wrote in those very experiences, including the deleterious effects on your young life that you describe—effects that have followed you to this day.

You may understandably want to know what could be gained by writing such violence into your life chart.

We would say that even given the answer we have offered here, the full reply can never be relayed in purely Earthly terms. Which is why every answer we give in this and all our books are powerfully interwoven with energy codes that your higher self receives, then passes on to you, as you are open to them.

In most Earth cultures, despite what people are taught by their family or community, each person's own intuitive desires guide them to work daily toward creating a fulfilling life of Love, Abundance, Peace, Joy—all of the things your spirit, body, and mind are made for. In this particular Earth life, you have been far more successful at all of these than you give yourself credit for.

There are many millions on Earth who have suffered what you have suffered, who never received an education or job training, who have no financial stability (even less than what you have at present), and who have never been able to move out of a violent environment, as they continue to recreate it over and over in new scenarios. New environments, same story.

Yet we would give them only a slightly different message than what we give you here today.

Which is, that it is nearly impossible to anchor higher Light into a desperate situation to the depth and extent that you, on a soul level, decided to anchor it, without being physically present in that situation, and knowing it intimately, as only an Earth human could know it.

This is not a task that we in the higher realms—even those of us who have lived Earth lives—can perform *for* Earth and her people. To do so would violate the free will agreement we abide by at every moment, permitting ourselves only the allowable exceptions. We absolutely respect your choice to live freely, without intervention on our part, except for those moments which your own vibration and commands create.

The causes and meanings of the life journey you describe are complex and multilayered, and we shall not delve into all of them here. But we would say that in your particular case, as in many cases, the man who played the role of father to you in this particular Earth play is a being you have met up with in a number of other Earth lives, and with whom you had an agreement in this life, for the aggressor/victim experience.

We can assure you that he feared and detested his role nearly as much as you feared and detested yours, and his. And that neither of you are truly an aggressor or a victim on a soul level.

If you could see the brilliance of your Light, the power and beauty of your soul and all it has birthed on this Earth over the millennia—if you could see your true form as you flow through the higher realms—you would never again doubt your supremacy, in this Earth timeline or any other.

You came into the life you have lived so far, even with its times of sheer despair and feelings of irretrievable loss, because you desired to anchor higher Light and higher forms of healing in exactly the areas you have yourself suffered in, and as fully as you have suffered in them.

This is not a half-measure, or a well-meaning gesture. This is a powerful sweep of higher intention that has and will continue to extend throughout time, cultures, and millions of lives.

*And how can that be*, you ask, *when I am not yet done healing myself, let alone others?*

While you are on this Earth, your self-healing will be ongoing, as you are able to raise your vibration many times over. What you are experiencing now goes well beyond healing as you understand it.

Your experience now has to do with Transformation of the highest order. It has to do with remembering Who you are while in a human body. And it has to do with anchoring the reality of your growth process into the vibrational reality of millions the world over.

This is a very tall order. The effects of your work—your very presence on the Earth, dear one—extend well beyond situations of mental illness and domestic abuse, extensive as they are. In fact these experiences, which occur continuously and globally, hold a more far-reaching and insidious density than even the war and terrorism you mention. Scenes of war are simply considered to be the more interesting and more obvious forms of violence, to the men who decide what topics will fill history books, and what will be discussed on the evening news.

**It is nearly impossible to anchor higher Light into a situation to the extent that you decided to anchor it, without being physically present in that situation, knowing it as only an Earth human could know it.**

It is so, that Earth has been subject to various timelines of wars and other forms of deprivation, loss, struggle, and conflict. Life on this planet has for millennia been subject to influences that guided Her into many dark experiences. And though we do not judge another's experiences—a planet's or a person's—we agree of course, that choosing the lighter and more joyful experience is always the higher path.

But that decision to experience Joy is made once one arrives upon the Earth. Before then, your choice may well be to encounter significant forms of darkness. Numerous Lightworkers are in fact warned by their Spirit teams and loved ones, before reincarnating, to lighten the load in their chart regarding what they have planned to experience in their upcoming Earth life.

You were told that this would be a steep path, that your life energy would pay a high price in exactly the forms of dysfunction, loss, and "dislocation" you describe. And you were told you would not feel very often that you belonged—not to the various groups of people you would meet, not to Earth life, and not even to your own body many days.

You came with soul understanding that all of that can be superseded with the inner realization of the Divinity—the power, beauty, and perfection—that you are. Yet that realization comes very slowly to the one taught early on about the sadness, anger, and feelings of the futility of life. To them, there is no way around this "reality," because that is all their caregivers knew, and all they know, until they discover other, higher vibrational realities.

We will not fill you with the popular phrases you know well already—that your habitual expectations and thoughts create your reality. (Actually, it's the emotions behind the thoughts.) That your vibration determines your outer circumstances, not the other way round. That you are a powerful co-Creator who possesses their own inherent decision-making, situation-creating power.

That you are always captain of your own ship, even on days when the opposite feels to be true.

You know all of these phrases and truisms, and they are not actively rescuing you from feelings of despair and helplessness. And we would say that much of what you are experiencing goes well beyond what a shift in outlook can offer, as your current outlook is encoded into the chemistry and neural pathways of your body and brain. And these can only offer the forms of coping and survival that they have acquired so far.

And so we will, via energetic transfer, flow to you now (and all who are open to such) vibrations that in an unfolding way shift both outlook and viewpoint, leading to new ideas, new solutions, and higher forms of perspective that lead to healing and renewal.

Even the idea that you do not have to be imprisoned by family or cultural trauma on any level leads you to those energy workers, realizations, inner shifts, and epiphanies that remind you of your soul's power to transform any situation you find yourself in.

## We prefer to call you powerful—someone who is able to create beautiful, Abundant, fulfilling forms in every area of life.

That begins with your beliefs about that situation, and which forms of Transformation you will allow. Many do not grant themselves very much ability to improve their lives. They will explain to anyone who asks, "If you hate your job, why don't you look for another one?" that they must stay where they are, because of this situation or that, which they have no control over, and so they are stuck.

We see this as we look out over the hearts of human beings, and find it difficult that all of you powerful co-Creating magicians would sell yourselves short on such a steady basis, even going so far as to defend the smallness and stuckness of your life.

One day our writer was speaking with Abundance author Ken Elliott, who wrote the wonderful book *Manifesting 1, 2, 3.* She described the various energetic and psychological traps that her father and his family had fallen prey to during the Great Depression in New York City in the 1930s. The hunger, the repossessions, the evictions. The grief, depression, and rage that gripped the parents, which their children tried to process and integrate into a far saner and kinder way of life, with only limited success.

She could feel even as she was telling Ken this story, that she was explaining why certain things are difficult for her. She also realized in that moment that she was doing what so many spiritual teachers caution not to do: investing in a Story, one written before she was born and inherited from family, rather than creating on her own from much higher vibration.

And she saw that she was lowering her vibration, and closing down possible positive future outcomes, by proclaiming this past as a powerful influence on her path.

This author Ken quickly caught on to this as well, and reminded her of that well-known phrase, "How's that working for you?"

In other words, Does it work well for you to point out the illness and imbalances of your family—physical, mental, or otherwise? Is it a positive moment, when you think about what you came from, and wonder how you survived? (Without feelings of thankfulness that you did survive.)

Your life is indeed a miracle, but not in the sense that you have only survived by a thin margin. It is miraculous in the sense that you are a powerful Light Being Who came to Earth with only the thinnest recollection of your ability to turn any situation around. You have chosen to move from horror, shock, grief, or rage, to calm, Peace, and higher wisdom, returning to the vibration of your higher self—sometimes, within minutes or even seconds.

And so we cannot quite agree that you lack certain inherent life skills. Even if this is true to an extent, you have other vital life skills others do not have, which you are not including in your inventory of where you are in life. Many of these abilities and insights would not have come to you without the particular path you have traveled. You would not have had the inner knowing or energetic resources to help thousands of people energetically, in your work and out of it, had you not walked the life path you have walked.

And so we prefer to call you powerful—someone who is able to create beautiful, Abundant, fulfilling forms in every area of life. One empowering method is to spend time each day visualizing and fully *feeling* that you already are where you want to be in life—the circumstances of strong financial income, wonderful relationships, excellent health, and so on—and enjoying the beautiful feelings of being there, as if it were already occurring.

We would also not agree that the phrases you have given considerable co-Creative power to ("emotional dysregulation" and "de-personalization," etc.) have properly earned their place in your thinking. You are far, far more than anything that has ever happened to you, even that which continues to affect and direct some of your thoughts and energies.

The power of the higher self outreaches and overpowers even that which appears to be a powerful self-concept, at any time in your life. This means, in other words, that how you feel and what you feel you are able to do are not always a correct description of Who you are and what you are actually capable of.

This is why energy work is so powerfully important, whether it comes to you through a book, a live energy clearing or healing session, or a video or audio recording. Or through the presence of someone whose higher self is actively working with your higher self to clear anything in the way of your being able to accept the full range of possibilities for your life.

Any child or adult who has suffered trauma in a third dimensional life has unconsciously opened up portals in their energy systems through which energy forms, entities, and belief systems flow, seeking to inhabit their heart-mind and etheric and physical bodies, in ways that easily fool them into thinking, "This is just who I am," when in fact, it is not who they are.

Your painful side—the aspect that feels it has been left out of the true flow, depth, and fullness of life—does not own you, but it will most assuredly behave that way. This is one reason why daily meditation time, energy healings, and energy clearings are so vital. These are badly needed for you to discover the true self, hidden deep inside the false self, built up by natural defenses, self-protections, energetic interferences, and cultural programming.

You are not the trauma you have suffered, and you are not the entities and energy forms that have entered your life energies in times of shock and vulnerability. And you are far, far more than any label intended to classify the results of your experience.

You are, in fact, the One who designed the life you now live. You came willingly, with an energy of excitement and positive expectation, into a world of conflict and chaos, because you knew that planting yourself into a domestic situation of fear and violence would give you the prime position from which to anchor higher Light into similar situations. This includes those larger areas of conflict in which people point technologies and other weapons at one another with intent to destroy.

You have experienced Joy, fulfillment, Love, and an inner Peace nothing could tarnish, and you will again. But currently, you are in the midst of an energy wave that appears to be shadow, and is in fact manifestation energy. This can be quite demanding to handle on one's own. It has its roots and intention in manifesting fifth dimensional energies in the human psyche. This is part of what you came in to accomplish, with millions of other Light Warriors.

Yet from where you now stand, it feels to be nothing but pure opposition.

## Your outer life is reflecting the shift into an entirely new phase of being. You are in a Void.

This is understandable, as it is a weighty, dense energy that is struggling to maintain the third dimensional status quo. Yet you and your soul family members are not allowing that to happen.

So that what feels to be an utterly personal struggle is anything but. When you are in your etheric body, while your physical body is in its sleep state at night, you are working with full awareness to adjust this resistance into higher dimensional intention and flow. And working subconsciously during your waking hours for the same goal.

This is a big job, not a small one.

And so your outer life is currently reflecting the shift into an entirely new phase of being, as you experience the uncertain feelings of that shift. What you are in is nothing less than a Void—that difficult and trying space-time of releasing the Old.

In the Void, you are using the life energy once required to maintain the Old to create the New. You are between forms of existence, and that is trying, to say the least.

To move yourself into what you desire for yourself, speak to the energy of the former life. Send it Love and appreciation for all it gave you (and all it gave humankind and the Earth). Thank your old life and your former ideas about Life in general. Yet realize you are now vibrationally Ascended to where you could never return to the old life. The energy building inside you will not permit that.

Your life energies are now centered in growth on a whole new, higher path. One where the Ascension of your physical cells and consciousness are opening to new forms of understanding—of how energy flows in the Universe, of how new forms are birthed (both ideas and outer forms), and Who you truly are.

Which is, a powerful Being who travels the many dimensions with ease, working with Light Beings of all shapes, sizes, and missions, to assist in Earth's and even the galaxy's Ascension.

Do not sell yourself short, due to what you suffered early on! We would not call you (or anyone) a victim in this great stage play you have been in, though the energetic influences you carry require you to label yourself that way.

We would prefer to quote here French writer Anais Nin, who wrote in volume one of her book *The Diary of Anais Nin*, "One does not have to remain in bondage to the first wax imprint made on childhood sensibilities. Once the deforming mirror has been smashed, there is the possibility of wholeness; there is a possibility of joy."

We send strong waves of higher Light to you now, to release from you the deforming mirror—all of the lower beings, dense energies, and interferences of any kind that have been working for so long to keep you separate from the joyful intentions of your higher self.

And we strongly encourage you to work with those capable of releasing you from the torment of your family line, as well as those energies that have crept in during your most vulnerable moments, in this and other Earth lives.

This is another reason why you have incarnated at this time— to release the influences, traumas, and energy interferences that have come to you in other lives as well, which this life's trauma has echoed and repeated, asking to be healed or released.

There are powerful energy clearings offered free on some websites. These are utterly priceless for their far-reaching ability to shift a person's energies from a hopeless and weakened state to an empowered one, if you are willing to allow that. Many are so used to the energy drain of those beings and interferences that inhabit their energies, that they mistake these for who and what they are. These are the subtle, invisible reasons for struggle that you refer to.

We assure you that that feeling and experience of struggle is not Who or What you are. To release this, you must be willing to release the old labels and definitions, though they seem only to be "telling the truth" at present. You must be willing to define yourself as a joyful Light Being, climbing out of the third dimensional constraints to remember your true form and essence.

Form the clear intention to do this—to experience Joy and fulfillment in a permanent way, one based on your own inner Light and connection to the higher realms, not on your present circumstances, and not on your past.

If you are able to do that, and to hold that intention every day, even in the face of emotional resistance that seems to own you, a new life will find its way to you, as you find your way to it.

In time, it will feel to be the only script you ever wrote, while still in the Peace and beauty of the higher realms.

# 3

# On Being Shut Out by a Loved One

*What is the nature of the blockages and the no-contact policy between my daughter and me, and what can I do about it? Or do I just have to live with it?*

*Although I have asked for her forgiveness many times, that I left her father and loved another man and married him, taking her and her brother with me, she doesn't want to accept it, and doesn't want to be in contact with me.*

*I don't even know exactly what she accuses me of. She said it was "wounds from the past."*

*She went through an emotional burnout and postnatal depression, and has done therapy and trauma therapy. But that hasn't led to "normal" contact with me, so far.*

*I've done countless Ho'oponopono prayers, and solved everything on my side, holding her in love and blessing her and her family.*

### *Is this just something I have to accept and live with?*

This is an excellent area to discuss, as so many are experiencing family and friend estrangement now.

Understand that children do not always see their parents as individual adults with interests, needs, and personal expressions of their own. And of course, parents often have trouble seeing their child as an individual adult, even when their son or daughter is well over the age of thirty.

Your daughter did not see you as a woman seeking to be honest about her feelings, her life path, and her strong preference to be with the man she loved, instead of the man she no longer loved.

Though this was an honest and brave move for you, your daughter, in her youth and inexperience, saw you only as one of the two pillars holding up her sense of reality, her inner and outer life, and her understanding of how life ought to go—even her understanding of how the Universe works. Then one of those pillars moved out of place, disturbing and upending her world, and her sense of sameness and safety.

And so, she reasoned that if her mother could change, and change her children's lives as well as her own life—anything in life could change. Anyone could present themselves as someone unchanging and utterly reliable in the way that children need and expect, then suddenly break that unwritten, deeply held law, and do as they needed to do for themselves, and expect others to adjust.

## This is an opportunity to learn what you could not learn in other lives.

Now, we do not say this to judge you in any way, for you were merely following your life path. And interestingly, your daughter has been doing the same—following her life path. Before incarnating, you agreed to experience this very situation together, and to deal with the resulting rift between you in ways that would bring each of you into greater understanding of certain forms of heart-based experience and soul growth.

You have also had past lives with your daughter, in which you were the one to release or never fully connect with her, rather than the other way around. And so this is an opportunity to learn what you could not learn in those other lives. It is not a cold form of universal karma—the Universe is not an unfeeling machine that spits out calculations and life results according to what one "deserves" in a punishing sense.

It is the completion of a cycle.

There are other forms of energetic interference that your daughter is experiencing, and this accounts for much of the depression and shock that have remained in her energies. So much of what she is carrying is not yours to take from her. She must come through her own growth processes, both for healing that which is in part inherited from the women in your family, in part a result of what she has experienced in this and other lifetimes, and in part what she came in to experience in this life.

If you have been saying Ho'oponopono prayer ("I'm sorry. Please forgive me. Thank you. I love you.") for both yourself and her, and blessing her and her family with Love, you have done what you need to do, in addition to asking for her forgiveness, which she may not be able to give you at this time. We would simply release her and allow her to Be—to choose the life she prefers, while you go on with your own life.

You made a brave departure from a life you could no longer stay in, taking your children with you, though they realized in that moment that they had little power in deciding how their lives would go. In leaving their father and moving out with you, they were not following their own preferences, but receiving an outer decision they had no influence on.

And now you have handed your daughter nearly all the power in the relationship, as if that would make up for your decision to exercise all the power in her life when she was a child.

This puts her in the position of being able to say "No" to you in a way she could never have said as a child, except energetically. There are many things that can make a daughter feel unsafe, insecure, or unheard in a new home situation. Having lost what she felt were her Choices—her voice, and her vote for how her life would go—she now takes whatever power she has to make sure you understand how much she suffered.

Her comment that she has cut away from you due to "wounds from the past" is naturally vague, because it wasn't any one thing you said or did that created this rift, from her perspective. It was the overall action of changing her life and her safety—shaking up her sense that all would stay quietly in place as needed, until she was old enough to move away from her home and her father in her own time and way.

The removal of a child from his or her father creates its own insecurities, even when that move is necessary, whatever the reasons. The situation can indeed feel traumatic and unyielding. It is a removal of the moorings that had previously kept the child from feeling alone, unguarded, and unsafe in the world. A new stepfather does not necessarily bring the same assurances, and can be a source of anxiety.

This is what she blames you for, more than anything. Not for choosing what made you happy over what did not make you happy, for that choice has empowered her to choose much that she has preferred in life, over that which she has not wanted. The blame is for removing the steady unmoving floor underneath her and replacing it with the moving deck of a ship that was headed somewhere unknown.

In time, she will come to accept that move as something she not only planned in her life chart, but as a moment that shifted her energies dramatically from one form of life to another. And that new path was not crafted for mere security and comfort. She understands what it is to feel shifted in dramatic ways that go to the core of the heart-mind and personality. She is capable of helping others who have also experienced this sort of shift.

**She can never give you enough Love and reassurance to lead you to where you will finally Love and accept yourself. That is your path to walk, and no one else's.**

When she is ready, she could work with others through effective energy work, though she would need to first come to the place in life where she realized her abilities and her life path, and she is not quite there yet.

In the meantime, your guides have been asking you to not obsess over this situation or to try to remedy it, but to *release your daughter and her family completely*, in body, mind, and spirit. She will never feel it is safe to reach out to you while you are trying to draw something from her—some reassurance that you did the right thing for her and her brother, as well as yourself, or some return to the relationship you once had.

That cannot be, for too much has changed. You would need to begin again, not as her mother this time, but as her objective friend who is willing to hear what she says, not in ways that you feel reflect upon you or your actions, but only in the objective sense of just Listening and Being There for her.

As she is an adult with a child of her own, and has released you from your mother role, you must, if you expect to be fully in touch with her again, also release yourself from the mother role. Release her from your energies, your expectations, your preferences.

You are in essence asking yourself for forgiveness for having shifted your children's lives in such a complete way—even more than you are asking for your daughter's forgiveness. Her cutting you out of her life is simply a metaphor for your own guilt and unhappiness. You are trying to solve that by feeling that if she could just forgive you and let you back into her life, all would be resolved. And yet, it would not be.

She can never give you enough Love and reassurance to lead you to where you will finally Love and accept yourself. That is your path to walk, and no one else's.

And so we would say, allow her her choices, as she once had to allow you yours! Respect her stance and her beliefs, and leave her entirely where she is. People do not generally do what you desperately need or want them to do. They do as they feel is best for them, or what their duty is, and tend to pull all the more away from those who impose an ego-mind (survival) need to have them behave in a certain way.

Love itself does not demand, push, or grieve when another pulls away. It allows and blesses, and releases the loved one. This is part of the path you came to travel, and a great part of what you are here to learn. Once your heart opens enough to allow your daughter her own life and preferences, even if they do not include you, you will release the grief you are carrying. Most of that grief is for yourself, and you are the only one to cure it.

Many are finding now that their paths have taken them down a road that some of their family members cannot accept, or that their vibration resonates at a level that some of their loved ones find difficult and annoying, if not outright untenable.

## Every Lightworker must accept that there are those who will walk out of their life in this time of Transformation.

This is one of the more difficult aspects of the Ascension process—the realization that you are not going to be able to take everyone with you. Some are damaged and see the world through a skewed lens that does not allow them to put Love before a family member's life choices, experiences, or beliefs. Others envy the Light they see in a loved one. And others worry unconsciously that they are not taking the same risks, and living the same very honest and authentic path in their own lives.

Again, this is not your journey. It is theirs. Every Light Being in human form must accept that there are those who will walk out of their life in this time of powerfully shifting energies and complete Transformation of body, mind, and spirit. There are those who will not forgive the forward movement of a loved one's path. They will seek to keep their loved one small, to keep them in safe viewing distance, and not out in the Universe exploring ideas they have no knowledge of or interest in, or do not approve of.

That is understandable. They are not ready for such. But you cannot hold yourself back so as to placate the pain or fears of another, or to try to make up for it somehow. That is their own journey.

And so, yes—release your daughter with the understanding that she is her own person, and not simply your daughter. Say any time you think of her, "I bless you and release you to your higher good now, in all dimensions, in all directions of time-space. I give thanks, as I now experience my higher good."

Is this difficult to do? Of course—at first. And then you begin to realize that the only person you are here to change, to work on, and to ask things of, is yourself. And so it is your own inner self and your own higher self which you must sit down and speak with now, dear one, every single day. Find out where the wound began that you are living out now with the woman who was once your little girl.

Ask your higher self to show you the origin of that pain, and how you may heal it. And by extension, help to heal those in your family, both ancestors and current members. For as you shift your own DNA, your own etheric presence, and your own cellular makeup, you help to heal all those in the etheric and physical network that comprises your Earth family in this lifetime.

And so, attend to First Things First—your own growth and healing. Say the Ho'oponopono prayer for your child self and your adult self, and release all etheric cords between you and this young woman.

Whatever her challenges, she is finding her own way, and of course, dear one, so are you.

# 4

# On Facing Earth Troubles and Disasters

*Planet Earth appears to be going through hell. War, destruction, poverty, starvation, terrorist attacks—these only begin the list of horrors.*

*Has the time arrived when humanity is able to digest the phenomenal reality of just how simple it could be to shift the Earth's vibration?*

*Is it time to enter the next thousand-year cycle? An age foretold with Peace and Light and beauty?*

This is one of the greater questions of your age.

For it has to do far less with when, but *how* Earth and Her beings may rise in vibration to begin experiencing a far higher reality than you have seen in eons of your time.

We would say that one of the reasons you are experiencing the dissatisfaction you feel with how Earth is functioning now, is that you are aware of your own ever-increasing vibration. Because of this, you have an increasing awareness of how beautiful Earth life could be, if the majority held a higher consciousness.

This extends beyond the current challenges of dealing with extreme weather and climate change, armed conflict, violence on the streets or in the home, and illnesses and disorders that you know intuitively have been cured, though the cure is kept hidden from the public. This issue extends into the entire realm of each person's soul purpose, and why you are here.

When you move into that issue, as you lift above the chaos that is Earth's current frequency, you enter a completely different realm.

For then you are no longer asking, *When will we get it? When will we finally surrender our guns for Peace, feed and house everyone, see the Divine Light in one another, and fall in Love with that higher form of life?*

At that point, you have left behind your attention to What Is, to outer circumstance. You have then reclaimed your magician's ability to envision, to think in terms of what you will create next.

You are, in fact, asking a far simpler question—one of the few you ever need to ask: *What did I come here to do?*

*How do I serve humanity's and my own higher good? How do I naturally live in the energies of Joy, Peace, and Divine Love, so that others pick up on the beauty of that, and aspire to live there also?*

**Call upon every heavenly help you can conceivably imagine, as well as your intergalactic families, and require their assistance at levels unknown since the Fall of Earth.**

Even as you and millions of others are asking those questions, Earth is now entering the next age or cycle on Her timeline, and it is an age that extends very far beyond the thousand years you mention. And to usher in this beautiful era of the Sat Yuga, as the Hindus call it—a time of unprecedented Peace, prosperity, progression, and beauty—you need not wait for things to improve, or wonder why things are moving so slowly.

We would call upon every heavenly help you could conceivably imagine, as well as your intergalactic brothers and sisters, and require their assistance at levels unknown and unheard of since the Fall of Earth into the third dimension.

And more than that, realize your own connection to these great beings! It is time to come out of the feeling that so many looking to the heavens have sunk into over the eons—this feeling that though you have cried out for help, none is coming to you.

Earth Herself cried out for help when the weight of this form of existence became too heavy, too painful, too damaging for Her to carry out any longer.

And the answer that came from higher realms was you.

You heard Earth's cries, and you volunteered to step forward and say "Yes," committing to living yet another Earth life on one of the most pained and troubled planets in the galaxy. You stepped forward with the mission of anchoring higher Light on the planet, in human consciousness, in the entire galaxy. All for the purpose of not only establishing Divine Love as the new normal for Earth life, but celebrating it.

This is why we remind Lightworkers (or spiritual seekers, Light Warriors, Starseeds—choose any label you like—they are all too small to hold your true vibration) that you are not passive recipients of what flows before you as you observe life on your planet, any more than you need be passive recipients of what is happening in your own lives.

As co-Creators, you are here to change or influence something that you see has low vibrational purpose and intention. You are here to realize each time you see a condition, thought, or emotion that is crying out for healing, renewal, or a new life, that you are the one who can lift it to a higher level, even when you are convinced that it was your vibration that created that condition in the first place.

**If you want to see more Peace in the world, you must exude that vibration as the New Reality.**

*This is why you cannot go it alone, dear ones.*

You are in a human body, and the frailty and limits of that existence are considerable, particularly as you walk the Ascension path. Everything unlike pure Love is now rising to the surface to be healed or transformed, while you experience cellular, heart-mind, and etheric Transformation.

For that journey, and for all Earth journeys, you need many helps, supports, encouragements, and inspirations. Call out for them, and demand them from your higher self. You will not be abandoned. You will be led to exactly what you need, if you will only ask for this assistance.

We recommend to many that they listen to inspiring, high vibrational music whenever they feel to be at a low frequency in heart, mind, body, or spirit, or simply as a part of their day. These can be found online on YouTube.com, on certain websites, or purchased as recordings.

We recommend reading inspiring books that encourage you to turn your thoughts and energies—your focus and *attention*—to Abundance, Joy, fulfillment, Love, and living out your life purpose in joyful ways. The best of these books will, as with the one you are reading now, hold higher energies that do the job of lifting your outlook to where you see yourself not as the passive receiver of Earth's current conditions, but as a powerful influencer. One who helps to set the tone for how the world sees itself, and what it sees as necessary, possible, and real.

Your vibration alone influences many thousands of people. You are even now beaming out a transmission of Light and higher energies that reach thousands of miles beyond where you now sit.

If you want to see more Peace in the world, you must exude that vibration as the New Reality. We strongly suggest that you release all need to watch anything that is not peaceful— to cease watching any film, television, news reports, videos, music (which often is not music, but chaotic entrainment) that portrays or describes acts of violence, whether between two people or between whole countries.

# Despite the images of violence and chaos, this is a planet experiencing far more well-being than disruption.

Even economic news that takes a downward turn can feel to be a form of violence, as your subconscious will be quietly calculating, as you listen to the news report or commentary, how many thousands or millions of people will be affected by a "sudden downturn in the markets." There is so much in that one phrase alone, oft-repeated in the media, that is intentionally designed to lower your vibration and set you into anger, hopelessness, and feelings of loss—that is reason enough to no longer listen to news reports.

We are aware that there are alternative news outlets, programs, and reports that are insightful on spiritual levels, and that seek the true nature of the issues being reported in the mainstream media. Yet carefully watch your vibration as you listen to these—are you heartened by them, or disappointed? Are you feeling empowered, or weakened?

If you are feeling anything that is not positive and strengthening to you, do as any sensible parent would do. If your child was watching something that showed violence or some form of struggle without resolution in sight—inviting passivity, desensitization, and helplessness on the part of the viewer—you would turn it off immediately.

We say this not to discourage you from knowing what is happening in the world, but to limit your intake of that information—and you live in information-obsessed times. Focus on mainly taking in only that which feeds you on a soul level, and not that which depletes you.

Dense or negative news will have a harder time wearing you down if you are in the habit of not listening any further than the first few sentences that introduce what is going to be announced or discussed. That is often all you need to grasp the basics of a situation. And often, even that is more than you are truly interested in. You have simply been mentally programmed to "need" to know what is happening everywhere, and to sink yourself into the hyper-emotional stance of most news reports, as if all of Earth's fate hung in the balance with that one story.

That is the sort of holding-your-breath-and-wondering-nervously-what-will-happen-next unhealthy excitement—a concentration on the low vibrational—that we encourage you to step away from.

It is vital—not just a nice idea, but vital—that you take time every week and in a smaller way, every day, to steep yourself in that which, for you, describes the New Earth. Go out of your way to find beautiful and inspiring pieces of music or artwork, inspiring films, quiet and replenishing time spent in Nature, time with loved ones, reading inspiring stories, or laughing at comedies or life situations, getting your diaphragm engaged in the process of expunging the deep emotions that lie buried there.

Just as it is vital to step away from consuming meat and dairy products, which are highly contaminated, very hard for the body to process, and come from violent industries that are harming your planetary climate and well-being, it is also necessary to step away from the toxicity of the digital environment. This means moving away from both the devices themselves, and the content on them. And to stop allowing them to define your daily life.

We assure you, despite the appearance of the violence and chaos the planet has been steeped in for millennia, on the whole, this is a planet experiencing more well-being than disruption. The trouble is, in modern life, you will not catch a reporter standing in a peaceful, remote valley, or at the top of a stunningly beautiful glacier or cliff, breathlessly reporting that "All is peaceful here."

Nor do they often shoot videos of schoolrooms and colleges were there are no dense or negative events occurring, or say much about peaceful negotiations between countries, or the millions who have learned to recycle or repurpose their refuse every day. The news industry is convinced that high ratings, careers, and top sales are not built on such life-affirming moments.

This is why the alternative media, often driven mainly by independent content, is so important. Even your social media is increasingly understanding that people are thirsting after beautiful and inspiring stories, far more than the pain-filled descriptions of violence or dire predictions.

## In your Universe, what you focus on and *call* Reality can only increase.

The question is, *Where will you place your attention, powerful co-Creator?* What story will you choose to concentrate on, as representative of the New Earth that you and millions of other Light Beings are busy making?

Will you allow the old power structure to not only continue to train your mind and expectations, but to control your emotions, beliefs, and expectations of the world?

Or will you strike out on your own and decide Who you are, remember what it is you came here to do, and concentrate on— *increase*, in other words—those Earth experiences you would prefer existed everywhere.

We encourage all Light Beings (and you are all such) to realize your incredible co-Creative power, which lives within you at all times. It is impossible that you would consistently look at your checking account balance or spreadsheet, for example, and give thanks and bless and praise that "reality," without seeing it improve in a short amount of time.

Never mind that your logical mind is saying, "But we've only got a small amount of money in there!" You have *chosen* to see the Abundance that is within everything, and therefore, also within the open co-Creative field that shapes your accounts, your wallet, your everyday life.

You have *chosen* to work with the energetic reality that is constantly open to being molded into some outer form, or renewed into a higher form.

In your Universe, what you focus on and *call* Reality can only increase. It promulgates, grows, extends to greater heights (or depths). It awaits your labeling of it and your feelings about it, before taking off in exactly the direction you have indicated, with your beliefs and expectations.

Yes, you are that powerful.

And if only two or three people in an entire city determine (particularly if they combine their focus and intention in a group effort) that pollution, crime, inequality, fraud, and toxicities of all kinds are now going to dwindle to record-low numbers in their town—this has a powerful effect. Experiments have been conducted over the past few decades that prove that exact idea. As does your own life.

And so, take your eyes off of what you cannot stand—you are not assisting others or taking full responsibility for your inner life by continually allowing your vibration to fall. If there is a situation you hear of that you would like to actively help or send Light to, then do so. But if a thing feels bigger than you, or feels unsolvable, let it go.

Hand it over to your soul, the Angelic legions, Creator God/Goddess, and say, "I give this to you. And I send healing Light that your Divine solution be made manifest in this situation, now and always. I give thanks!"

Then go back to being a positive human being who inspires everyone they meet.

Go back to singing your song, and doing what is joyful to you, for Earth's sake. For this you came.

# 5

# On Supporting a Romantic Partner in the Ascension Process

*I would like to know what we can do for our partners who are still a good match for us in our lives, but who are not consciously on the same path to Ascension, and who struggle with the intensity of life changes and shifts, especially in their nervous system, thoughts, and beliefs.*

*I have been calling upon the Helper of Transformation and the Helper of Relationships for indirect intervention. Any attempt to directly address any issues tends to put my partner off, and activates his defenses.*

We are very glad you have asked this question, as so many are challenged by this issue. Especially now that millions of increasingly spiritually aware people are realizing that they must either release their relationship due to the changes they are going through, or find a new way to make the old relationship work.

It is natural to feel a bit done in by the intensity of life's challenges. And many have no conscious spiritual reference point. They do not know or believe there are helps available to them, including a wonderful, loving, wise Spirit team of guides, Angels, and higher self who intimately know their life chart and life mission.

Without that assurance and understanding, daily life can be a very lonely place indeed.

All of us in the higher realms seek to make ourselves known. We spend much energy and focus on the Earth plane, because we are wanting you to know that you are *never* alone. Yet it is hard for an awake-and-aware partner to see a loved one struggling to understand challenges that to them seem to have no rhyme or reason.

We would say, that if you can value your partner's path in the sense that you know it is perfect for them at any one time, that can save you from feeling that they are not where they should be right now, and that it is costing them a great deal. For most assuredly, it will look that way.

Yet "not all those who wander are lost," as the great writer Tolkien once put it.

It is easy to feel that someone is on the wrong track when they see life differently than you see it. Many see life in purely outer terms, and will share ideas and beliefs very different from your own. This becomes even harder to watch, when they appear to be struggling.

The reason your partner is put off when you attempt to address the issues of his life or belief systems is that he does not connect your words and ideas with any real outer solutions.

As a naturally compassionate and aware person who loves him, you want to be an active support, and you already know that tools such as meditation, visualization, affirmations, tapping, and declarations can be of great help in resolving outer situations. Even before a solution is found, Peace of mind can be found in focusing not on the problem but on the solution, believing it exists and giving the issue over to one's higher self and the Universe.

To someone raised to "solve their own problems," these do not appear to be practical tools that deal with the issue on the level where it began (energy). They seem only to be indirect pleas for help, or nice ideas that are irrelevant, and don't lead to real solutions. They look more like inaction, rather than action.

Because many situations involve other human beings, sometimes no amount of outer action can solve an issue, because the other person refuses to comply with another's wishes. Often, only a focus on heart-based energy (or just letting go of the situation) can shift another's attitudes, actions, or beliefs.

## People relate strongly to the images we hold for them.

And so you might want to simply address the energy of this situation. Image him coming into a realization that the Peace-filled, meditative way of problem-solving would be of great help. Visualize him calling in higher wisdom, and placing himself in the center of the energy of a solution, allowing the form of that to evolve. Doing this quietly will be a thousand times more effective than speaking to him about meditation, affirmations, or speaking to his higher self.

Explaining what your partner can do to help himself is not so much a demonstration as an intellectual argument, and he will take it as such. He may also mistakenly believe that you doubt his ability to solve his own challenges without your help—a skill that most men pride themselves on.

See if you can image him sitting quietly and meditating, or spending time in Nature, or speaking during the day here and there to his Spirit team and seeking answers, rather than reacting to life emotionally or argumentatively, and pushing against circumstances (which only sinks one further into "problem" energy). You will be assisting in his growth far more than if you were to get him to try a spiritual resource via your suggestion.

People relate strongly to the images we hold for them. They pick up on those ideas etherically and subconsciously, which gives them time to "try on" the energy of an idea and see if it feels right to them. Their Spirit team, meanwhile, can sail in on the images you are sending your loved one, as that line of communication helps make their voice and presence all the more clearly known to the one they are assisting.

Many have found that imaging someone as being well, no matter how ill they may be, at the very least lifts the emotional energy of their loved one, and assures them quietly that wellness is possible.

## Honor your partner spiritually as well as in other areas.

Imaging someone as very financially abundant—and comfortable with that reality, not embarrassed or concerned about it—is also very helpful. It is far more effective than trying to counsel them on how to spend or invest their money— something we do not advise, unless they have asked you to advise them on that!

Imaging an exhausted, overworked parent moving to a job with fewer hours and simpler responsibilities (or more fulfilling ones) and bigger pay is also a wonderful gift to give someone. Imaging a struggling student acing their exams and always knowing the right answer in class, speaking with confidence and clarity, is a beautiful gift to that young person. (Whereas, saying, "You need to study harder!" can either build further resistance to study, or be guilt-inducing—a very low form of motivation.)

If you value all other aspects of the relationship, you will need to honor your partner spiritually as well as in other areas. We assure you, he has had lifetimes in which he was spiritually aware. He is learning something from his current forms of beliefs that would not come to him otherwise. And soul growth comes in all shapes, colors, and sizes.

Allow him his path, as you would ask him to allow you your path. (You would feel unhappy if he did not.)

Let him wander. He is not truly lost, any more than you are, dear one.

# 6

# On Releasing Old Karma and Living Karma-Free

*In this transition to the fifth dimension, will every Earth-incarnated soul be fast-tracked to the point where they have resolved all past karmic debt?*
*Will the move to the fifth dimension onward incur no further karmic debt?*

Y ou are correct in realizing that life at fifth dimensional frequencies (or higher) does not have the phenomenon of karma or other forms of accumulated density. There is a flow to life, and an underlying compassion and intention of Divine Love, rather than the "stuckness" of the ego-mind and all its survival-based distractions, fears, and insecurities.

As you move into higher frequencies, you will not need to physically die in order to end your Earth life. When you are ready, you will leave—easily and consciously walking out of your body to return to the etheric. Or you may prefer to move on to another form of life, or another planet. But you will not experience the aging, illness, and death known to those of the third dimension.

To live at the fifth dimensional level or higher also means that there is no need for the kind of density that creates karma and other debt in human life. Not for growth and evolvement, and not as a natural outcome of living in a dense and chaotic environment.

Earth's and humanity's evolvement into fifth dimensional frequencies and consciousness are often expressed by individuals' declarations that karma is "over." You will hear people saying that they are determined not to accumulate any more karma, that they are releasing themselves of old karmic ties, and the weight of unresolved density from this and other Earth lives. And that they have made the commitment to grow in ease and joy.

They have released the painful path in which they end up owing themselves, another person, or the Earth an apology.

**The accelerated growth made possible by the rigors of Earth life has made life on your planet a much sought-after role in your Universe's great stage play.**

There is no "fast track" out of karma in the sense that you mean it, for that is not necessary. You will find as you move beyond the third dimensional construct of acting, saying, or being something that lives in density and good/bad duality, that all situations naturally seek a resolution. Upon returning to the etheric once their Earth life is over, each person views the events of the life they have just finished. These flow past them in a way that shares the emotional experience of each person in every situation they have lived through. They can then begin planning how they will resolve these old issues.

This is in fact why so many return to the Earth plane—to fulfill a contract with another in which old grievances are evened out, old misunderstandings finally resolved. They may have played the role of aggressor in one or more lives, while another played the role of their victim. They then work out with that person, once they have both returned to the higher planes, "This time *you* will be the aggressor, and *I* will learn what it is to be on the receiving end of that."

This is not a preferable form of soul growth, but it was for thousands of Earth years the form of growth chosen by those who have pushed forward to experience one Earth life after another.

You may wonder, *Isn't this, on a soul level, unthinkable? To come to Earth over and over making the same mistakes, with only small progressions made each time? Or none?*

We will say, first, that third dimensional Earth life is not for everyone. And yet, the accelerated growth made possible by the rigors of Earth life has made life on your planet a much sought-after role in your Universe's great stage play. Few, upon returning to the higher realms, regret having ventured out to play yet another role in that great drama, though they may regret certain words or actions, or lack of them.

The journey of resolving and dissolving old karma begins when your own soul growth calls out to you while you are still in the higher realms. Your soul then works with you and your higher self to seek out a future life path that will lift your current vibration to a new level of awareness and responsibility.

At that higher level of empathy, you very consciously ask that all you have harmed in this or any life forgive what you have done or said. You also very consciously forgive all who have harmed you in this and all other Earth lives, in all dimensions, in all directions of space-time.

**Asking for forgiveness, extending it to yourself and others, and dedicating yourself to service are beautiful ways to dissolve the heaviness of what you have experienced.**

You have been directed by many of the world's major religions to believe you get only one life on this planet. As a result, for centuries it has not occurred to the majority of humanity that you need to release and dissolve old karma, rather than bringing it with you into the next Earth life. That time is over now.

Asking for forgiveness, extending it to yourself and others, and dedicating yourself to a life of service—*being* the Love you have sought to know in this and all your Earth lives—are beautiful, life-affirming ways to dissolve the heaviness of what you have experienced on this planet, in different forms over many centuries.

This is not beyond you, and it is part of your path into fifth dimensional life. This is your choice now. Will you seek to redress and right all wrongs, whether committed outwardly or etherically? You may find it very helpful to write a letter by hand on special paper to all those you feel have wronged you in this or any Earth life (whether you have conscious memory of those events or not), forgiving them for all they have done, and declaring there is no density between you and them any longer.

In that letter, also ask for forgiveness from all those you may have wronged in this or any Earth life, including yourself. Ask for forgiveness and release, thereby dissolving all density between you and them, on all levels of existence.

After writing that letter and reading it aloud several times, we would then burn it. This releases it to the ethers and your soul, and the souls of all those you have written to. All obligations between you and them are thereby released and dissolved, in all directions of space-time.

**You might want to write something such as:**

"I, [your full name], hereby ask for forgiveness for anyone and anything I have harmed in any Earth life I have lived, in any time-space dimension, in any and all situations.

I now extend forgiveness to anyone and anything that has harmed me, in any Earth life I have ever lived, in any time-space dimension, in any and all situations.

All is now dissolved between us, in all forms and in all directions of space-time. I fully and freely release and forgive all of you, and all my past life roles and actions, as you fully and freely release and forgive me.

All of us go to our higher good now. There is no further density of any kind between us.

All soul agreements, contracts, vows, bonds, and oaths made between me and all others are hereby ended and dissolved for all time. All is well.

And so it is!"

Tell your Spirit team that if something still remains for you to do inwardly or outwardly to dissolve all karma between you and another, or the Earth Herself, you need to know what that is.

But suffering further for past wrongs—no. That was never a requirement, except that Earth's density while in third dimensional frequencies created a form of living in which suffering, and evening out past deeds by suffering as you had made others suffer, was accepted as the (very low vibrational) form of learning.

Karma does not accumulate in the fifth dimension. Persons in that frequency vibrate at a level of good will that makes it unnecessary to harm another in any way. Density does not follow anyone from one Earth life to another. Misunderstandings are played out in peaceful forms, or erased due to the good will of both parties. No heaviness need be retained in a culture where there is no abuse of humans, the Earth, animals, plants, trees, the air, water, soil—all beings and all life lives at Peace with itself and others.

## You will find much to challenge you in this New Earth. Yet these will be joyful challenges.

That is the vibrational place at which all life begins in the higher dimensions—as Love embodied. You are that now, certainly. But once fully in the fifth dimension (for you have already begun to exist there), you will feel even more than see the higher frequencies we speak of. You will not tolerate constant left-brain chatter, nor make decisions based on beliefs in scarcity, competition, insecurity, fear for your or another's survival, or narrow-mindedness.

It will not occur to you that taking a risk on a new idea might result in serious losses, for in that higher vibrational life, you know that all things can be made new again. That there is no loss, and that because every aspect of your life is always reaching to experience and express your higher good, all is well.

It will not occur to you to eye another as a competitor or a threat. For you know that all are family, and all are seeking their own and everyone's higher good. You will know that there is plenty for all—no losses, no scarcity, and no chance of "losing" to another.

It is not so that life will lose its thrill, its interests, or its challenges. You will find much to challenge you in this New Earth. Yet these will be joyful challenges. They will not rob you of the chance to view another as a fellow traveler on the way to ever-increasing enlightenment.

You will seek not so much to win or to have, but to realize and to inwardly grasp the wisdom, higher Love, Peace of mind and heart, and fulfillment you have spent many lifetimes seeking—usually (as you were too busy trying to survive) without even realizing it.

In the fifth dimension, Peace is created in the world as each person declares enough self-Love and self-empowerment for themselves. And so as always, everything in Life begins in the heart, and cannot vary or wander far from that.

For you are such stuff that dreams are made on, as the bard would say, and your little lives are rounded with a sleep.

Or they were—for in the fifth dimension, there is awakening, which you are even now beginning to experience. Note how those visions carry you forward! Call out to them, to make themselves real through you. Do not "wait" for anything or anyone. You are here as co-Creators to know and experience the New Earth in very real and brilliant terms.

Once you have created that clear focus, intent, and expectation, there will be no stopping the miracles you will begin to create.

# 7

# On Releasing an Attachment to a Loved One

*As I watch everything fall apart around me— people dying, going away, marriages ending in a lot of brutal painful ways, I still feel such an attachment to someone who was a catalyst for much of the pain I carry.*

*Is it necessary for my advancement? After years of trying, I am wondering, how do I let go and accept that this person is not a part of my future, and truly be free to start a new path?*

We would say, that it is important to remember that your life experience is based on many things—and that many of the energies, ideas, preferences, and feelings you carry are not *you*, exactly.

As we note in other chapters, each person carries a powerful legacy behind them of ancestral energies, traits, patterns, belief structures, experiences, traditions, tendencies—a long list of influences that most people mistakenly believe themselves to be free of, because "that's all in the past. And I'm the progressive one in my family."

Indeed, you may be a progressive thinker, yet still be burdened by the trauma experienced by those in your family. That suffered by the children in the family, or by the women, or the men. Those tendencies will pass on to you uninterrupted if allowed to. You are not yet so far out of the third dimension that its many traps and patterns are beyond your experience.

Your immediate family likewise handed on to you certain tendencies, mental and emotional traps, addictions (these come in a wide range of guises), and beliefs about the nature of reality. These are so natural to you, having been taken on by you from the womb onward, that you are rarely even aware that they are there. They tend to determine the shape of your day by deciding what you believe to be possible—about work, health, relationships, and other areas—because they shape your beliefs and self-concepts.

## You exist in the world as a bundle of influences and presences.

Your culture and all its various forms of programming are another source of patterning. The media is a programming tool, and used for little else, though certainly, other higher and more positive messaging and energy codes do get through to the masses. Yet far more influential has been the programming to "do as you are told" and "view the Universe this way." Though that is now on the wane, that was still the case as you were a child and evolving into an adult.

Past life experiences, and past life associations with certain persons whom you have met again in this life, are another area of influence regarding how you feel about life, and how you view anyone you love in this lifetime.

Chances are great that you are also not the only presence inhabiting your body. It is the rare human being who does not have entity attachments or interferences of one kind or another—an ancestor or deceased family member, a lower entity or deceased person seeking an energy source and physical body to inhabit. Other interferences include energy forms—thoughts and emotions which may not have a self-aware consciousness, yet still inhabit whole parts of your energies, whether you created them or not. Earth-based and ET implants and interferences are also still a part of the human experience at present.

And so, due to upbringing and family influence, as well as media, government, education, and their various energy transmissions, your culture and ancestors, your past life experiences, old soul contracts, and energetic interferences of different kinds, you exist in the world as a bundle of influences and presences. Most of these are not your own. You would never choose to carry them if you were fully aware of them.

Human beings are rarely aware of all that is working on them and stealing their energy each day, each hour they are on the Earth, and these beings and programs are aware of that unawareness. It gives them all the more room to inhabit as they please, and to direct your actions, thoughts, feelings, reactions, beliefs, and inner ethics.

Yet all is not lost, regarding how you feel about life, whether in relationships, physical death, loss and abandonment, lost love, or any other topic that is pulling your energy down to where you feel lost, except for those times when you anchor yourself in the presence and loving attention of another.

## You chose to come forward at this time not to feel bad about life, but to feel joyful about it.

As we have noted elsewhere, there is no pain that is necessary for your evolvement, though many have chosen to learn in that way. We would take active steps to release the idea that pain and struggle are necessary for advancement of any kind. Even tough physical exercise, grueling academic study, and the rigors of raising children can have their own kind of joy, in the perseverance and focus they require.

They can also be motivated by Love, not merely self-discipline or duty.

There are many ways to step up and reclaim more and more each day the beautiful Divine Being you are—the person you came to Ascend into while still physically on the Earth. You chose to come forward at this time not to feel bad about life, but to feel joyful about it. The conundrum comes when you are given the message, while still at a young age, that romantic Love is the point of life. You are told that you should seek a Love that makes you feel at home in life in ways you have never fully felt before, and that assures you how wonderful you are.

The training human beings receive from films and popular songs are two powerful influences. They affect most people starting very early in life, informing you that to love someone romantically is the pinnacle of existence (unless one is fighting in a war, and even then, you will note that a romance is often woven into the war story). This tends to keep people trapped in drama, their hopefulness never quite fulfilled.

That is the Love you are seeking, but we will say that that is not a romantic Love. The Love that offers complete assurance is based in the high heart, and begins first within yourself, for yourself. Otherwise you will forever seek it outwardly, which always leads to disappointment at some time or another. Romantic Love, though it offers some forms of fulfillment, is not meant to define or fulfill you. Expecting such will only lead you to blame yourself or the other person for not providing Love fully and in ways that fulfill your expectations indefinitely.

You are the one permanent fixture in your life, dear one, and no one else. You as the representation of Divine Love in human form. All else will fall away, in its time.

You have been taught to seek after and to worship outer forms, whether that comes in the shape of material wealth, fulfilling work life, or fulfillment from romantic Love and/or family life. And all of those things are fine and beautiful in their own way. But they are not the true heart of what you are seeking.

They are individual, outer expressions of it, but they are not the core, and they are not lasting.

Even a highly evolved person can fall hopelessly in love with someone who is not quite right for them, and who leaves at some point, because things are not working out. Or who is wonderfully right for them, but who leaves this Earth far sooner than ever expected.

Outer situations are only outpicturings. They are holographic forms, and not anywhere near so "real" as everyone assumes. They shift and fluctuate, and after a while, fade or transform. The person who does not know self-Love and self-supporting kindness will find that "the one" they have decided will finally fill that gaping hole within them can only offer them so much Love and reassurance.

In this Universe, everything constantly moves forward at a great pace. On the Earth at present, that pace is quickening far more than in the past. Change is the only constant, as they say, except that it occurs many times faster now than in Earth's past.

Now, we will return to our earlier point for a moment, as this is where things become rather interesting.

You can set mind and heart to a particular point of focus, a particular area of creation. But until you consciously begin the process of releasing all that is not you, you will still be steered to a great extent in the direction determined by those energies that are inhabiting your physical and energetic space, as well as those who have programmed you since birth to behave in certain ways—to "follow the rules."

You will also be steered to fulfill a deeply unconscious family legacy, which goes back many generations, to times when the rules of life were far rougher, more violent, and more struggle-and-lack-oriented than they are now.

This is why the various forms of energy clearing are so necessary now, whether from meditation, or through an energy worker who is skilled in releasing or neutralizing ancestral influences, as well as trauma, dense beliefs, emotions, and energy patterns. Some are also quite skilled in releasing past life curses and oaths, ET implants and energy interferences, and other forms and presences that are stealing or siphoning off your life energies, and influencing you in ways that are not healthy and not representative of your soul and your authentic self.

You are also, as many Lightworkers and empaths are, a highly intuitive person, sensitive to the energies of others. You carry the energies of those you have wanted to heal, protect, guide, or assist in some way, unless you did so with conscious awareness of not taking on their energies in the process, or have since consciously released those energies and cut all etheric cords between you and them.

For the intuitive, this tendency to pick up on and take on the energies (including the pain and sadness) of others begins in infancy, and even in the womb. Many realize early on that they are not like the rest of their family, and that they must take on the energies and beliefs of those around them, or be left out in the cold on one level or another.

When you fall in love, you likewise take on the energies and outlook of the other, and it is vital that you release those energies on an ongoing basis. Do this even while you are involved with someone, and absolutely once you are no longer involved with them. Your emotions can become enmeshed with their presence, and you must withdraw your energies from the other person, as you also pull their energies out of yourself.

## Look into the situations of your life, and begin to ask for Joy, fulfillment, adventure and beauty.

You can also use meditation to call back to you your own energies each day, and to actively cut all etheric cords between you and another. Use the image of a giant pair of scissors, or a large sword, and visualize cutting through all etheric cords connected to you. Or ask Archangel Michael to use his Sword of Truth, Excalibur, to cut you loose from all energetic ties above, below, and all around you.

What you consider now to be pain that has come from your having loved and lost someone, is actually only an expression of a pain that was already there. It has simply been revealed to you, coming up to the surface from the subconscious, and seeming to be new, when it is anything but.

We advise practicing self-Love and diligent self-care on all levels, to anyone struggling in this way. Decide each day that "this day is for me, to Love and care and believe in myself," and do as many kind things for yourself as you can think of. People in pain don't always eat very healthfully, or exercise enough, or keep their surroundings in order, all of which can help tremendously in feeling more peaceful and cared for. They also unconsciously spend time with people who are not positive for them, or isolate from others, or do things they don't really care about, thinking they have no choice.

Look into the situations of your life, and begin to ask for Joy, fulfillment, adventure, and beauty. You can create these if you take some time to ask what it is you really want, when you stop feeling that you are At a Loss, Left Behind, and Alone.

Ask yourself, each time the pain comes up, "What is feeling this pain and loss doing for me? What is behind it? Where did it come from to begin with?" You might want to do the story writing exercise we recommend at times, which is to get a pen and paper and to write at the top, "Who are you, and why are you here? Why are you putting me through this?" Then switch the pen to the hand you do not usually write with—the nondominant hand—and write the answer automatically, letting the real story come through all on its own.

Abbreviate words where needed, as the handwriting may not be very neat. But let the answer come forward. You may hear from your child self, a past life self, someone with whom you have had a soul contract for some time, or someone inhabiting your energies.

After you have answered those questions, ask yourself, "Is this pain filling a void of some kind? If I feel empty—if I am mainly noticing pain and loss right now, why is that?" And again, let the answer come up, either on paper or in your heart-mind.

You can dissolve all soul contracts. That is a choice you can make. You can dissolve all etheric agreements that are pulling your energies down. You can do it in meditation, and you can create an actual Statement of Release, in which you release all soul contracts to anyone, made and agreed to for any reason, in any space-time and in all dimensions. You have that choice.

We would say that you are fully capable of releasing this pain if you are willing to do so, once you decide that you love yourself more than the pain you are feeling. And once you decide that your life is precious and sacred, and to be lived fully, every day, whether a lover or spouse accompanies you on the journey or not.

You can realize, with the help of a counselor and energy healer, or with affirmations, meditations, or declarations (or all of these), what it is you truly desire in life. That you are here to dream big and to live even bigger.

And that there is no one person who hands you your Joy, your fulfillment, the self-Love and approval you have yearned for since infancy—except you, led by your higher self and soul.

# 8

# On Learning from Conflict and Adversity

*Has Source, via souls, reached a limit on what can be learned and experienced through adversity? Was adversity and conflict on Earth ever truly required?*

*Will there be any other "school" in the multiverse that specializes in the adversity and conflict that have been present on Earth? Or will these aspects no longer be a requirement for learning in this Universe?*

We shall start with your first question, regarding whether Source, via (Earth-based) souls, has reached a limit on what can be learned and experienced through adversity. We would say that Source, expressing itself via human experience, has no further use for learning through adversity in Earth life.

You have heard third dimensional Earth life referred to as a Great Experiment. One in which Divine Beings—which is all of you—came to Earth to experience what some call a "university of hard knocks"—a boot camp or survival course. None of these terms go far enough to sufficiently describe the challenges you have endured while in a human body.

This is why we have such admiration and thankfulness for your bravery in having chosen to incarnate upon the Earth so many times. Many of you have been anchoring increasingly higher levels of Light and enlightened consciousness into the Earth and into human life, over many centuries.

## Adversity and conflict were never a necessary requirement on your planet, for soul growth or any other objective.

For this is not only a place where challenges are taken on for purposes of expansion. It is a place where events and challenges can diminish your spirit into fragments, which must then be healed and rejoined once you return to the higher realms. Yet it is also a place of renewed hope for your Universe, of unfettered growth, and of deep and resonant higher learning.

The adversity limit you speak of was reached some time ago. From there it was simply a matter of entering the era which you are entering now, which is the Sat Yuga, the age of Peace and prosperity, of fulfillment and intercultural understanding, of unity amongst individuals and groups, and of desire for open, transparent communication, high intentions, and respect for Lady Gaia.

Adversity and conflict were never a necessary requirement on your planet, for soul growth or otherwise. Earth was allowed to fall, in this free will Universe, and allowed to remain in a lower frequency of emotion, thought, belief, and entrapment of every kind (social, economic, spiritual, physical, intellectual, governmental, and so on) for thousands of years.

Duality (viewing life as good/bad, right/wrong) was an experiment you chose to experience, which fell far out of control. You have been waiting on your own awakening, and on the

Universal mechanisms of astrological currents and events that have been introducing the Sat Yuga. The planetary soul of Earth Herself also called out for help, as humankind took a deliberate decision to stand up and require its sovereignty. This occurred even before the vibrational opening could occur for galactic/etheric intervention to assist in Earth's Ascension back up the scale of evolvement.

Yes, there are other third dimensional planets in this Universe, and they can also be difficult, dense, taxing places to spend one's time, though Earth is an extreme case. Again—there is no requirement heaped upon any planet in a free will Universe, except that it not be allowed to usurp the free will of others, or to destroy itself to the point where other planetary bodies, star systems, and those in the etheric would be harmed as a result.

(We speak of this Universe rather than of the multiverse, which is a colorful and varied panoply of lifeforms, universal laws, and intentions that are too far-reaching in forms of experience to include in this discussion.)

Adversity can be allowed to occur in this Universe, so as to create an environment of learning, for purposes of accelerated soul growth.

## Even your controllers and their scientists are realizing that the way of adversity and conflict has seen its day.

Divine Will can find expression in any Universe that is not self-destructive or uncontrolled to the last degree. Freedom is one thing; self-destruction—allowing a planet to blow itself up, for example—is quite another. In your Universe, that is no longer permitted.

There have been a number of incidents on Earth in which nuclear missiles were deployed, including being sent to or from the United States. Sometimes the missiles do not make it out of the silos—a number of military personnel have spoken openly in the media of seeing craft appearing in the sky and some capability in those ships disabling the missile silo or launch in one way or another, to stop the launch from occurring.

In instances when the launches have occurred, the nuclear arsenal was disengaged from the missile and set into a controlled explosion far out into space where it would harm no one.

In your current timeline, there have been limits on how much chaos would be permitted on Earth. And now, having hit a dead end with that form of destruction, even your controllers and their scientists are beginning to realize that the way of adversity and conflict has seen its day. Destruction or avoidance of it no longer influences life on Earth as it once did.

You may ask, *Is humankind realizing this on a mass scale?* We would say that there are mixed results in that area at present. And yet—the energies pouring onto the Earth now are of such a magnitude, of such an increasing depth, power, and resonance, that all that is seeking healing is coming up to the surface—even those beings once consigned to the shadows.

Yes, you are finished with conflict and adversity. It has been on the wane in Earth life for a while now, and will continue to fade.

That form of life need no longer be the way of learning on the Earth.

Earth beings made the decision to experience life and themselves on those terms for millennia. And now, with that experiment ending, they have decided instead to know Peace, to learn in Joy, to experience being the Divine Love that created them.

# 9

# On Helping Loved Ones Deal with the Ascension Process

*I've been fairly relentless over the past few years with my personal healing journey, my spiritual growth, and my reconnection to consciousness and our Galactic family. I can sense when Ascension energy waves are coming in now, and take everything in with a sense of wonder. But that's not the case for everyone.*

*My cousin is experiencing the same amount of energies running through her body as I am. Prior to her Ascension symptoms showing up, she hadn't been curious about the journey of healing and spiritual growth.*

*She has been feeling these symptoms with a lot of unease: strong nausea and depression to cite a few, often laced with a sense of fear, because she has a hard time understanding what is happening to her on a cognitive level. I try my best to calm her down and explain what is also happening to me, but am not sure how effective my words are.*

*Do you have any words of wisdom we could share with our loved ones, who may not be ready to hear all the esoteric terms yet, but who are clearly undergoing the path of recalibration to self and Source—that they may hear them, understand this path, and feel safe?*

*In the case of my cousin, going to the doctor would probably result in her being given antidepressants, and that doesn't feel like the most appropriate course of action at this time.*

This is a crucial issue, as billions around the world are experiencing their Ascension in myriad ways that some days leave them feeling elated and energetic, other days confused and concerned, and often, ill or exhausted.

You ask for words that could substitute for terms such as "Ascension symptoms." We would say, it would not be unusual for you or anyone to point out that solar winds and solar flares are affecting all life on the planet, as is climate change, and that the world's structures—economic, political, social—are shifting very quickly now. And that all of these shifts and others are powerfully affecting all life and all consciousness, include physical well-being.

Even someone who does not usually discuss spiritual growth is able to notice the shifting political and cultural scenes and Earth changes. They are able to see how people are in a state of nervousness, anxiety, and depression many days, as evidenced by social media posts and commentary. Most are able to read an article on solar activity and its effects on the Earth and humanity.

Millions are witnessing the shift in not only climate and planetary processes (extreme weather, earthquakes, volcanic eruptions, etc.). They also see that millions around the world are reacting to these shifts with feelings of uncertainty, and sometimes, panic.

All of this, as well as the powerful energies flowing to the Earth now, have made it a demanding enough time for a conscious Lightworker. Someone who has little to no conscious connection with their Spirit team, and no inclination to meditate and ask for guidance, will find it even more confusing.

Your explanations of what is happening in the world and to humanity reach your cousin on a cognitive level, while what she is experiencing is happening on a physical, emotional, etheric, and intuitive level. This means that your words, however well-intended, will not necessarily reach those aspects of her being that are most fully experiencing the shifts you describe.

Words are one way in which people communicate, and one form of sharing information that many learn best by. But you will find increasingly that you live in an era when people are moving away from language and left-brain labels as a way to understand life.

As you have noted, your cousin is finding it overwhelming that she is taking in large, weighty realizations and understandings that reveal aspects of her spirit and soul to her. These are coming in at an alarming rate, and in ways that the brain's cognitive functions cannot easily categorize. Whole aspects of her personhood are shifting her perspective from a mind-centered experience of life, to a heart-centered one.

And in that shift, much that has been buried deep in her heart—in the subconscious, and in the soul—is coming to the surface, demanding to be heard, healed, or celebrated, and integrated with the whole.

## Your best explanation of how someone can be at Peace in the midst of unprecedented transition, is the peacefulness and reassurance of your own presence.

It is difficult to put this phenomenon into words for someone who has not fully grasped yet that they are nearly all spirit, and only a tiny part physical. Most people weigh and measure their life by outer accomplishment, appearance, social roles and status, financial means, family background, work or career. Even the poet and the prophet over the centuries, for all their high-heart intentions, have often viewed their lives this way, for this characterized life in the third dimension.

Your cousin is now realizing that this outer shell is not her life. It is the outer aspect of her experience, not the meaning of it. Her spirit is calling to her to look up—not only at the night sky, where some of the lights visible to her are ships—but to look up inwardly, and to realize her life actually exists at a whole higher level. She recognized this as a child, but came to disregard it under the cultural training nearly everyone undergoes.

Most assuredly, your words are effective in calming your cousin, though not because of the work of the words themselves. All writings that have uplifted, comforted, and inspired humanity have done so by transmitting higher energies embedded *in* the words. Words also carry their own energies, which they have been imbued with by use and belief over time.

Though the mind is able to relay some meanings to the spirit, it cannot hand on meanings that are beyond its ability to grasp. That is solely the work of energy transmission. That is the world of energetic intention, heart-based meaning, and higher knowing. In third dimensional life, that has not been the kind of knowing taught and encouraged among the masses.

Yet now the veils that once hung between humanity and higher knowing have faded and dissolved.

Now that Earth is moving into fifth dimensional life, you need not think purely in terms of using words to convey meaning. The ancients and pre-ancients knew this. This is why you see such intricate carvings of symbols—hieroglyphs, pictographs, and other images on the walls of caves, pyramids, and great temples around the world. The stones and chambers of the pyramids themselves still offer potent energy transmissions. The ancient and pre-ancient peoples knew the power of these energy transmissions, and the universality of symbols that humanity relates to on a soul level.

They communicated beliefs, experiences, messages from beyond Earth, with images that were symbolic of higher meaning, or that described histories, myths, and enlightened experience, via energy transmission.

## There is no verbal explanation that can exceed the power of another human being's loving, kind, supportive presence.

When you speak with your cousin or anyone, understand that it is your presence—your energy—that they are reading, far more than your actual explanations. You can if you wish find ways to discuss or explain what is happening in the world in ways your cousin will mentally grasp. But she is likely to only take these in as interesting ideas that are not too relevant to her life. They will not filter down fully into her life experience unless she resonates with the energies inside the ideas.

Your best and highest explanation of how she can be at Peace in the midst of this huge, unprecedented transition, is the peacefulness and reassurance of your own presence. This includes the kindness and encouragement you offer. She is able to pick up on the beauty of your inner grounding, to feel your inner knowing that despite feeling physically ill or emotionally tangled up some days, it is possible to know that at the Source of it all, All Is Well.

There is no verbal explanation that can exceed the power of another human being's loving, kind, supportive presence. Not that you are wanting to walk this path for her. But that you are offering what support you can by being there, hearing how she is doing, and perhaps now and then, suggesting that she spend more time in Nature with bare feet on the ground, letting Mother Earth take from her the toxicity and confusion coming up at this time.

Human beings have gone to Nature for peaceful resolution, wisdom, comfort, and grounding for millions of years. There is also an abundance of beautiful, peaceful, higher vibrational music available. A search for "high vibrational music" or "crystal bowls" for example, on YouTube, will bring up much that can lift one's spirits and be a comfort. Nature sounds—sounds of the forest, the rain, or the ocean—can also be found there, and are also perfectly attuned to the higher aspects of the human spirit.

Though we do not fully diagnose anyone's overall condition physically or emotionally, we can relay that her Spirit team are saying that things are coming up about her family background and other issues that she needs to discuss with a therapist or counselor, even if only once a month. These issues are far more challenging to resolve on one's own, and another's input, once the right counselor is found, can be very helpful in sorting through thoughts and emotions that can feel overwhelming otherwise.

She also needs to work with an experienced energy worker who will help clear the presences of current family, ancestors, and energy forms that are present within her DNA—inherited traits and trauma, as well as current and past life traumas.

Much is coming up that, once resolved, released, or integrated, will reap a rich well of wisdom and heart-based understanding of the human condition. It will also assist her own Ascension process, as she is able to support and encourage others.

Again, your own example here is priceless. Be open about your own path. When you are willing to talk out the questions you have with a counselor or trusted friend, or to spend time in Nature and in meditation, or to listen to peaceful music, to pour out feelings and frustrations into a journal or through creative expression, or to take special quiet time for yourself, you are demonstrating for your cousin and everyone around you that you are walking calmly through these transitions, and being kind to yourself in the process.

Your willingness to be a kind and positive support to her, to demonstrate Love by feeling and being Love in a heart-based way, is the most powerful form of assistance you can give to your cousin or anyone, and the most effective.

This demonstrates that the center of this Universe—Source Energy, Creator God/Goddess, the All-That-Is—is Love itself.

That is the final word in all experience, in all feeling, all thought and realization, and most assuredly, in every Ascension journey.

# 10

# On Discovering Your Life Purpose

*I have been wondering what my life purpose is, for a while. I know one part of it is being a mother, however I feel like there may be more to it than that. I have done different things to try to help determine what my life purpose may be, but nothing concrete really comes up for me.*

*For example, I have often been told that it is related to what you really wanted to do as a child or were very passionate about as a child. Using this approach, I don't get much of anything, as there really was nothing I aspired to be when I was a small child, other than maybe "famous."*

*I've also heard to look at what you are currently passionate about. This also falls a little flat for me, as I don't have strong passions, other than maybe working on being the best version of me that I can be.*

*I know that sometimes it is the "small" things we do that have big ripple effects, so we never really know the full effects of how or when we do something, because it can have big ripple effects and impact so many others. And so, at times our "purpose" can be offering support for others. Yet these are actions that we may view as small or maybe not very impactful.*

*How do we determine what our life purpose is, or if we are on the right track to finding it?*

This is an important question, and one we are asked often.

While our words are an answer to your individual question, they apply to all in a general sense. The energies we are transmitting in this particular chapter are made to reach each individual in the way that he or she most needs regarding life purpose, according to where they are on their path right now.

You are correct in what you are nearly saying—that someone could live their entire life and not have a clear image or phrase that sums up their life purpose. And we would say, that it would be unusual to have just one clear phrase or image, as most people's life purpose encompasses many areas of their lives and involves many aspects of their spirit.

By your description, life work is actually what you are speaking of when you say "life purpose." Yet your life purpose is actually far greater than any work you might accomplish. It is a very definite purpose, though like most Light Bearers, you have not yet grasped the many layers and aspects of it.

You are correct in saying that serving others, no matter how small the act of service may be, is a large part of your purpose on this Earth. This is why we often speak of life purposes, plural. You are many things, and you have come here to do and to be many things.

Childhood interests and areas of fascination are inner indications of things that don't so much encompass a person's inner purpose, so much as demonstrate parts of it. And so you might feel real joy when hearing beautifully produced orchestral music, because you pick up energetically in those compositions certain frequencies that you know, deep down, are powerful in healing certain ailments of heart, mind, or body.

You may be drawn to certain beautiful images in photographs—mountains or streams or waterfalls in different parts of the world—because unconsciously, you remember visiting those sacred sites in other lives, and performing powerful rituals and ceremony there.

You may notice certain forms of architecture, symbols, or artwork, and realize inwardly or even unconsciously that these originated in certain Galactic civilizations that lent their expertise and insights to those who created these structures. At times, those Galactics were the creators.

Even the slightest interest in something—a color, a shape, a sound of any kind that you resonate with intuitively, is telling you Who you are and Why you came.

## You came to shift life on Earth vibrationally to a far higher level. That is your purpose.

You notice that we are not connecting any of this to a specific job title or area of work. It is a beautiful and fine thing for anyone to connect passionately to an area of work that they throw their life energies into, and perform with Love and complete focus. The world would not be the same without a Dr Jane Goodall, a Mother Theresa, or a Nicola Tesla, for example.

These fine people dedicated their lives early on to changing the status quo and moving the situations they were observing to a far higher vibration, whether in service to science and energy, animals, or human beings.

We would say that the world owes them great thanks for all they have contributed. But as fine and extensive as that work has been, it cannot begin to cover their true purpose, which is far more extensive and far-reaching than even 18-hour work days could encompass.

They came—and you came—to shift life on Earth vibrationally to a far higher level. That is your purpose, and you could no more avoid it or "fail" to do it, then you could suddenly disappear in a puff of smoke.

We will agree that to be involved in pursuits that are engaging and creative—to feel to be a part of a team working together on a common cause, or to work on your own to fulfill a long-held vision—is a beautiful thing to experience. And if that work offers you the environment or opportunities you have dreamt of—the chance to travel, or to use advanced technology, or to facilitate healing, or to teach, for example—all the better. For part of why you came was to enjoy the experience of discovery, and to acknowledge your innate gifts, and to develop them.

Yet you did not come here mainly for that experience. The ego identifies with labels and categories. It needs to have a particular role, a clear Who and What, before it can be even slightly satisfied with the status quo.

That has its purpose, yet you will find some of the most unfulfilled people in the world have fulfilled successfully some of the most glamorous, fascinating, well-paid outer roles. Pop star. Astronaut. CEO. College president. Senator or parliamentary representative. Film actor. Bestselling author. Groundbreaking surgeon. Energy healer.

These are things that one does, yet they are not what any one person actually *is*. That can never be fully encompassed by an outer role, even though it might be partly expressed through one. What you really, fully *are* goes much, much deeper. And therein lies your higher purpose.

## If you are looking for work that is fulfilling, have you thought about serving others in some way that is meaningful to you?

Though your child self could only guess at what was truly important—it seemed to be those famous people she saw on TV—your inner self always quietly knew that there is no race to run, no need for stress or even a named role. No need for costume, make up, announcement, or adhering to any one social class. Cultures require those so that they will know who should receive some respect, who should receive a great deal of respect, and who should get none.

It is an empty venture, to define oneself by what one "does," and—though your question was not that extreme in its area of focus—we do not recommend it.

And now we will ask, *If you are looking for work that is fulfilling, have you thought about serving others in some way that is meaningful to you?* You will need to take your focus off yourself. For your soul and higher self have wisely chosen not to give you specific preferences or mental images as you look for your life work, and your greater reason for being here.

*Can you take some time to "forget" yourself, and to focus on how you can help someone in need, or someone simply needing a smile, a bit of respect, or some encouragement?*

If you truly desire positive outer action, we would look into either volunteer or part-time work in which you are assisting those who need help of some kind. This might be at a homeless shelter for people or animals. It might be holding newborn babies who have no one to hold them in a hospital, because they have no parents. It might be working in a community garden for those who have no food to eat otherwise. Or answering phones for a help line of some kind.

In other words, we are throwing ideas out here and there, not because you should immediately and intuitively engage with any of them, but because we would like you to explore. To take on the great adventure of finding out what you can offer—what you have to give to others or to the Earth Herself.

Again—this is not all about action. Even if you were to be struck tomorrow with some illness that kept you bedridden for the rest of your days, you would still be fully performing your life purpose, and in beautiful ways. For the vast majority of that purpose, for any Light Being, is simply anchoring with your very presence on the Earth the astounding energies pouring into the planet now.

By holding and living these energies, and integrating them into your being, you are assisting Earth and all of humanity—all life on the planet—with the move into those higher frequencies that will embody and demonstrate fifth dimensional life.

And we could not possibly think of a bigger job, for one born on the Earth at this time.

So that instead of asking, *What should I do, and how should I start doing it?* we would say, offer yourself the opportunity to appreciate what you are *already* doing, and doing beautifully.

You mention motherhood as part of your life purpose, and it most definitely is. Yet you are probably not realizing that each day that you go through the movements of being a kind, patient mother who is appreciative of a child's special Light and uniqueness, you are anchoring that mother's Love into the Earth, into Earth life, into human consciousness, in beautiful and empowering ways that are quietly felt round the world.

That creates a healing wave of energy that covers all it encounters with encouragement and reassurance, and there is no stopping it, as it joins with like frequencies to eventually create a tsunami of Love and appreciation around the Earth.

Is there something more important than experiencing the Love that you are, and expressing that to yourself and others? We would say no, for even enlightenment flows out of that kind of existence. But it is understandable that you would love to do something that brings you satisfaction and fulfillment in what is called "work" on your planet.

And so, we would advise you to begin with giving to others—to help anyone in any way that you can. From that, something beautiful will grow. And even if it doesn't flower into an outer form of paid work that you carry on with for years at a time, you will still be giving, in that beautiful and irreplaceable way that thrills the heart and fulfills the soul as nothing else can.

And so, there is much for you to live and experience, Light Bringer!

We send our Light, that the way will be lit up for you and all those seeking as you are, in beautiful and encouraging ways.

**11**

# On Releasing Relationships You No Longer Resonate With

*My concern is that I have had certain friends in my life for a long time—ten to fifteen years. I feel that I am usually a supportive listening ear for them, or going the extra mile to attend to their needs.*

*I often feel this way in all my relationships, which sometimes makes me withdraw and retreat [to preserve my energies]. I also suffer from physical pain in my lower back and limbs.*

*My question is, though I have already pushed most of my longtime friends away, is this a useful tactic?*

*I don't feel that I am gaining much from these relationships. This situation seems to coincide with my physical pain, which I feel constantly. I am needing some advice in regards to friendships and physical upheaval.*

There are many ways to get one's needs met in any relationship, and constantly seeing to the needs of the other is one of those ways.

It is also a way of not revealing oneself to the other person. If you are constantly busy taking care of others, it is unlikely they will even bother to stop and ask how you are doing, and to see where they can assist *you* in some way. Most likely they will settle into the pattern that your energies, words, and actions have established—yours being the dominant vibration in that connection.

It is kind and good-hearted of you to want to be supportive of friends—to be the listening ear, or to assist them in some way. But what you describe is a caregiver relationship, such as a nurse would extend to a patient. That is not a personal relationship, so long as you are always the counselor and supporter, and they are always the receiver of that caregiving.

Though your needs were met to a degree by that sort of arrangement for a while, it seems that now you have reached a place in your path where taking care of others no longer strikes you as positive or satisfying. That is understandable. These people may not even have come to you expecting to be taken care of, but once you took on that role, they happily accepted it.

What often happens in this kind of situation, is that the empathic healer/caregiver takes on the needs and life challenges of those they are caring for. They unconsciously take on the heaviness of whatever the other person is carrying, which that person has not yet managed to resolve or heal on their own.

This is where getting your own needs met comes in. For you took on those energies in the hopes that it would feel like you were being loved and appreciated, while saving yourself the trouble of feeling the sadness one can feel at seeing another struggle as they deal with challenges.

One day you realize that your back and your limbs can only carry so much. Because unless it is your own child you are caring for (till they are old enough or capable of caring for themselves), you are carrying too much. Your body, heart-mind, and spirit were not built to live another's life for them, even if that means you must sometimes see them struggling.

Even if you fear they will not love you unless you do all you can for them.

## When you work to solve another person's problems for them, you lift them out of the very situation they created to evolve further.

You have now isolated in the hopes of rebuilding your life energies, and in the hopes of finally creating clear boundaries between you and others. It is understandable that you have released those who came to see you only as a problem-solver and caregiver, for as we say, those relationships were not a two-way street.

Losing your life energies to another, while taking on the heaviness of their life energies, really solves nothing. Far from solving another's challenges, you have only created more of your own. And you have unknowingly interfered with their path.

They created those circumstances on a higher level to learn from them. When you work to solve another person's problems for them, you lift them out of that chance to evolve. They must then create more challenges to gain wisdom and evolvement from.

You are correct that a natural-caregiver-helping-a-needy-person connection is not a true friendship. It is nothing like what your heart is really asking for, which is a real meeting of heart-minds. A connection of life purpose, interests, or temperament that brings you into equal footing with another, regardless of who carries the dominant vibration when you are together.

You are seeking a connection between two people who recognize that they are walking a path of evolvement that has everything to do with inner growth and realization, discovery and adventure, and nothing to do with someone being rescued.

When you meet someone who is of similar goals and interests, your vibration and theirs may seem to mix and line up quite happily. In that moment, everyone is on equal ground. This is a solid meeting of two individuals, each safe in their own vibrational space. Boundaries are clearly in place, and everyone is taking full responsibility for their own lives. That is a moment of fertile ground for creating a true friendship.

At the center of any real friendship is honesty—the kind that assures each person that neither is so blunt and brash that they will say anything that pops into their head. Nor will either of them pretend to be happy with the friendship if it doesn't suit them anymore.

In this (grace-filled) crisis point you have come to, you have realized that the rescuer/rescuee connection is not helpful, not fun, and not necessary. If you wish to help others, seek ways to do that in which you also are fed by the situation, not taxed or drained by it.

True giving from the heart, from a sense of Joy, always gives back. There is a sense that All Is Well, that the Universe is giving back to you in ways you cannot even name yet, and gifting you with a restful night's sleep as well.

When you over-give, particularly to those who are well able to take care of themselves, you are rarely energized or left feeling blessed and enriched by that connection. You may also worry that your advice will not be followed.

When you judge that a friend or adult family member is no good at taking care of their life challenges themselves, and worse, they agree with you, you are enabling, not empowering them. They are quietly agreeing that they are too weak to take responsibility to solve things on their own, and would prefer that you do that for them, as that is easiest for them.

### Your journey now is finding positive-thinking friends who will agree with you that each capable adult has their own built-in capacity to resolve their own challenges.

Allow others to stand up and do for themselves. In doing so, you learn a new way of relating to others. You simply listen when they say how they are doing, and when they speak of challenges, you encourage them by affirming that they are on the path to resolving everything happily and smoothly.

When you meet someone new, see them as capable—hold open the possibility that whoever they are, they can perhaps give something to *you*. You are tired at the moment, and needing a place of Peace to relax and feel at home in. You do not need more challenges. Your journey now is to find positive-thinking friends who will agree with you that each capable adult has the built-in capacity to resolve their own challenges.

Encouraging self-empowerment is one of the greatest gifts you could ever give anyone. That, and your simply being the example of someone who lives in joyful, fulfilling ways. They will seek to find out how you have arrived at such a place of fulfillment, and if happiness means anything to them, they will follow suit. That is true liberation and inspiration.

Regarding the physical issues, we would encourage you to look into therapeutic massage, acupuncture and acupressure, and whatever you can do of a daily yoga or Tai Chi practice. We say this because we can see your energy, and the energies of many millions who carry a similar need to care for others. You have for years carried many energies that are not your own.

The back will ache over those conditions, and the limbs will follow suit, because etherically, you have been carrying whole worlds on your back. Not only the immediate etheric energies of those you were kind to, but the energies of their families, ancestors, and past life patterns, even soul patterns.

That is too much. You have seen how some caregivers will fall into ill health, sometimes even serious illness, because they are carrying the toxicity of perhaps thousands of people they have met over the years.

They mistakenly (and often unconsciously) believe that taking another's pain from them is the way to move them out of a painful situation. It is not. Rather than removing an interference, they themselves become one. And they injure themselves, taking on life energies that are not theirs, when their bodies, minds, and spirits are not built for martyrdom.

## Extend Love and acceptance to the child within, and to the adult who cares for that child. Say encouraging things to yourself.

The therapeutic body work, and however much yoga you are able to practice, will do more than help you release physical pain and tension. They will shift your etheric energies in ways that retrain your etheric body to be free of carrying the energies of others.

Many have found it helpful to put a golden bubble of Light all around themselves, particularly when they're out in a crowd, at work, or at a social event. Crowded places can be difficult for empaths, as they pick up intuitively on the energies of everyone they walk past or speak to. Even a dinner party with a few friends can be demanding, if you are not keeping your boundaries clear and in place.

Remember that you are not here to rescue others—that is not your life purpose. You are a healer by instinct, and highly telepathic and intuitive. But your job is far more to transmit, to broadcast a message and a vibration of Love to the world and to all you meet. To offer an inner resonance more than an outer action—that is your real contribution. From there, others discover their own strength to resolve and work through and learn from their own challenges.

Nurture and be kind to yourself now. Perhaps in your family, as you were growing up, the only appreciation you ever got (or the only relief from criticism you got) was by doing for others. Now is the time to do for and appreciate yourself.

Extend Love and acceptance to the child within, and to the adult who cares for that child. Say encouraging things to yourself—compliments and supportive statements of belief—"I know you can do it! You've succeeded at that before, and you will now! You are irreplaceable, just because you're You."

And remember that of the people you came in to Love and care for, you are right at the top of that list. Unless you are caring for one or more small children, you are always your first priority. That is your first responsibility.

Release all beliefs that tell you otherwise, and be who you are! What makes you joyful? What makes you glad to be alive? Answer this fully now, and allow yourself to live it!

That is your job now, dear one, and you are the only one to do it.

# 12

# On Living Through a Dark Night of the Soul

*I have been experiencing great changes since 2012, and am exhausted by it.*

*My life is rough, and I'm tired. I feel like I have no one here, and it's heartbreaking. I'm in a constant emotional battle. I try to rise above it.*

*I don't know who my biological parents are, and it's frustrating. It keeps coming up, along with my son being sentenced to prison for life without the possibility of parole, my daughters being abused, and my having no money at all.*

*I encourage myself daily with exercise, sun-gazing, eating healthy, and staying positive.*

*I offered Love to my community, to the children who are neglected, and that backfired. I don't know what to do, but to only rise above it, and not complain, and keep fighting and waiting patiently for relief.*

Y ou are understandably exhausted, dear one. No one could experience what you have over the past few years without feeling drained and taxed by outer situations, and the inner revolution that they bring.

We speak of revolution, because that is what you are experiencing. You are also on a higher level anchoring higher Light into these situations for the entire planet, just as Lightworkers all over the Earth are doing.

It would be nearly impossible for you not to feel a loss of inner strength from even one of the situations you describe, let alone the combination of them. And so we will look at your life energy to explain what is happening, in the context of your particular life path, in ways that all who read this can also relate to in their own lives.

For one, you are carrying the burdens of others out of Love for them, because they are neighbors or family members or other loved ones. You don't want them to suffer, to have to walk the difficult or nearly impossible road that life seems to be demanding of them.

And yet each person is a fully active part of every situation in their life. They would not be experiencing what they are experiencing, if their vibration and view of reality were different.

That is true even of the children you speak of, for they came into this world already carrying a vibration from past lives, as well as a soul presence and intention for what they wanted to learn and grow from in this life. They then began picking up other vibrations while still in the womb, and while being raised in their family and social setting.

Anyone on a path of hardship may feel that they have been abandoned by the higher realms. Yet though that is their path at present, if they wish to change it, they are able to do so, even in the still-confining last vestiges of the third dimension. All are still self-determining individuals. So that if your daughters wish to end the abuse they are experiencing, they are able, out of sheer will and determination if nothing else, to create better lives for themselves. They are able to release the belief that there is no way out for them, and no alternative living or working arrangements possible.

*All* is possible, in fact. All things are possible areas of creation, if one remains open to the outer forms those ideas arrive in. It is only the human mind that has a desperately narrow frame of reference for the field of possibilities in any one situation. The mind sees what it believes to be a list of possibilities for a situation, then too often shuts down, refusing to believe any other ideas or solutions exist.

You are able to encourage your daughters to love and believe in themselves to where the idea of allowing someone to abuse them in any situation becomes increasingly unthinkable. This is so, even though what they saw occurring around them in childhood led them to naturally accept abuse as adults, as if that were inevitable.

This is not to lay blame, but to draw a line connecting any person's vibration—their emotionally driven thoughtforms and beliefs, which are mainly unconscious—and the life that they build for themselves outwardly.

## Peace cannot show itself outwardly until it has been established in a person's vibration inwardly.

Your son will not, on this Earth timeline, spend his entire life in prison, as prisons will be eradicated over time, once they are properly seen as the inhumane and utterly ineffective punishment they have always been. Even in prison, if he is able to adopt a feeling of nonresistance to his situation—if he can allow and accept it, and find the beauty in the present moment, whatever that might be—he can rise above what most would consider a very difficult situation. Certain books and meditations may help him reach this, and higher vibrational music, if that is permitted where he is.

The author Eckhart Tolle has reported that some persons in prison have written him that his book *The Power of Now* was very freeing for them inwardly. They report that they can see a bit of the sky from their window, and know that freedom and openness still exist. They connect with that reality inwardly and vibrationally, and in that way participate in it.

This is the only way forward for nearly every human being.

Most feel trapped or caught by one circumstance or another in life, as they find at some point that they are not free to leave a marriage or a job, or a neighborhood or living situation that is not right for them, as quickly as they would like. Or they feel trapped in a body that does not function fully. Yet until they are able to create an improved life condition, that is the path they walk.

Creating Peace within, whatever a person's outer situation, is really the only way to create it. Peace does not exist in outer circumstance, though it can be expressed there. It cannot show itself outwardly until it has been established in a person's inner life. Even when someone "by chance" wanders into the peaceful atmosphere of a Buddhist temple, for instance, in the middle of a loud and busy city, they can realize that somewhere in their vibration, they have taken a stand for experiencing Peace—and the Universe has answered them.

You can image your son peaceful and fulfilled, supported by friends and kind people, whatever his outer circumstances, and doing some form of work that is fulfilling and positive for him. You can visualize him being safe and treated well, and you can inwardly see him walking free from that prison while still a young man, and receiving whatever help he may need spiritually and psychologically.

Hold those images close to your heart, and practice them every day. Holding thoughts of him suffering, isolated, fearful, or unhappy will not assist either of you. You must release the addiction most human beings have to drama, and to lines of thought that spiral further downwards and only end in greater despair.

Release it, for this tendency is not who you are! It is the result of much mental programming and inner energetic presences that should not be there.

Likewise, image your daughters standing strong and tall in their own space, using their voices fully and in positive ways, speaking their Truth, and believing in themselves as individuals who have the right to expect fair, kind, positive treatment. Image them as women who would never stand for anything below that complete respect.

Applaud and encourage them each time they draw a clear boundary. Encourage every move they make, however small, to let go of those who treat them badly. Visualize them realizing why they unconsciously created those situations, and what they are learning about themselves because of them.

## You are the active co-Creator of every situation in your life.

Along the way, know that all your children are learning more from their current situations than an easier and more peaceful situation could have ever given them.

You cannot know the entirety of their path or their plan for soul growth in this life, or what they are releasing or healing from past lives. And so you cannot judge a thing in their life as Good or Bad. You must release them to their higher good. Know they are living their own lives in ways that are important to them, even if for reasons that none of you can see at present.

Regarding your own situation, we would eliminate phrases such as "having no money at all" from your thought and speech. What you say, think, and believe to true, or even jokingly state to be true, you tend to pull into your experience. This is more than the Law of Attraction. This is one of the Laws of Creation.

For you are the active co-Creator of every situation in your life, and you are the only one who can stop yourself from needing to identify with situations such as having little or no money. Far better to identify with always having *more* than enough money. Affirming aloud every day, at least 25 times a day, "I always have *more than enough* money," or writing it out by hand many times a day, will shift your vibration in a whole new direction. The subconscious is always paying attention to your descriptions of your life, and repeating exactly that situation outwardly.

You see how your children's lives have been molded by inner expectation, beliefs, and thoughtforms that have not served them. By listening to your own thoughts and spoken words, which claim to be simply "telling the truth" about your life, you can see how your thoughts and ideas have shaped your own life in ways you are not happy with.

We agree that you are rising above all that you describe, and that is wonderful. We would now go further. Steep yourself in high vibrational music (search that exact phrase on YouTube), and allow yourself times of quiet times of meditation each day. Picture often in your own imagination whatever it is that would make you most joyful now. (You can picture this outwardly also, if you enjoy making vision boards.)

We would also ask daily, "How can I serve the higher good of others, as well as my own higher good?"

Put yourself in the position of wanting to offer Love to others, as well as to yourself—the kind of support that doesn't need to be needed, doesn't need to be thanked, though that can be a learning process in and of itself. In that moment, you are offering from the heart. Not from the left-brain mind, which demands to know "Why?" so often and is rarely satisfied with the answer.

You are offering service not from society's expectation that you are here to be "successful." Or from even the inner expectation that you cannot be happy until outer challenges are solved and put to rest.

You are offering in those moments support for others and yourself in ways that are life-affirming, that come naturally, that are not viewed as interferences or judgments, but as simple affirmations that each person is special, brilliant, unique, and much-needed on the Earth at this time.

And so your path has become one of not forming judgments of Good or Bad. Not feeling that all is lost or that you have no more inner resources to fulfill the path before you, with no more energy and hope to lend your loved ones. Their paths are their own, and must be followed and developed by them alone. And they are strong enough to accomplish this. So release them, and allow that.

And then—branch out a bit. Write yourself a handwritten letter in which you pour out all you can no longer carry—the daily stresses, the sadness about your son, the worry for him and your daughters, the feeling of not being appreciated or understood by your community.

Write it all down, read it a few times, and then burn the letter. Release it to the higher realms, to be filled with Light by your soul and higher self, and transmuted from pain to wisdom.

## You are able to remake your life.

Then write yourself another letter. Write of the things you would love to see and do in the world. The work you would find most joyful and fulfilling, even if there's no job title for it. The kind of people you would love to meet. The experiences you would love to have—travel or study or adventure or just plain fun. The kind of financial Abundance, Peace of mind, and feelings of fulfillment you would love to have. Write it all down, and put it under your pillow, in an envelope addressed to you, your soul, your higher self, and the Universe.

Write at the end, "Universe, I am here to be joyful and fulfilled. Show me how to do this now. Whatever it takes for me to release the burdens I took on so young in life, show me that now, or release them through me. Heal me of all that holds me back from living my highest and most joyful life. I call upon you now, and I request and require Divine Solutions and Divine Wisdom from you now, on this and all other matters in my life. I give thanks!"

Then sign and date the letter—you may wish to mail it to yourself, and open and read it again at a later date. Know that it is reaching the highest forms of intelligence, Love, and awareness in this Universe.

Know that it will reap change for you, as you allow that to unfold, listening inwardly each day to your Spirit team of Angelic guardians, guides, and higher self. Sit with them each day and ask for their wisdom on any issue you wish. Or simply ask, "What do I need to know?" Then listen and learn to discern their voice or whatever inner images or feelings rise to the surface. Specify that only that which is of Divine Love and Divine Light speaks to you now.

You are able to remake your life, dear one. You are able to create forms of income that are satisfying, steady, and more than enough. The Universe awaits your orders, and also awaits your coming into steady alignment, mentally and emotionally, with that which you desire to create.

So demand to learn how to do this now, as you fill yourself with those books, music, films, and relationships that build you up, and remind you of your own inner strength and beauty, your own co-Creative ability.

You know intuitively how to do this. So claim that ability now, and move forward in Joy. We and your soul and higher self are with you, at every moment.

# 13

# On Overcoming Food Addictions

*I've come so far in my life, through a bad marriage to self-sufficiency and hearing my Angels.*

*I'm moving forward financially and feeling stronger, except I cannot beat a lifelong food addiction. I see a good therapist, but I'm sinking fast into my disease.*

*How do I move forward?*

Wewould say, that seeing a therapist can be extremely helpful, if they are someone who is able to positively support your particular life path. Yet there is always more to be addressed in anyone's energies and experience—far more than what is happening with a person emotionally or psychologically, and more than what any one therapist generally has the skills to discover.

Most therapists, unless they are also skilled energy workers or psychics, do not have the skills to tap into unconscious patterns that have remained from past lives, for example, or to spot entities or forms of programming in your energies that are masquerading as personality traits, family traits, or psychological blocks or trauma.

There is a great deal in human beings that can never be answered fully without traveling through the etheric reality— viewing the etheric blueprint of that situation to see what else is involved.

There are also neurological patterns, some inherited and some developed from childhood, that influence addiction patterns, and can hold them in place quite stubbornly, despite much outer assistance and inner work done in therapy. There are doctors who are able to assist in this regard, because they are skilled in reading energy as well as the neural pathways that predetermine certain drives and compulsions that affect both mind and body.

There is also group help available. The success of the 12 Step programs owes much to their having been built on spiritual discovery and self-examination of those motives, fears, and preferences that hold people in enslavement to the forces within themselves that are feeding off of the addiction cycle.

**Though it is not necessary to name every form of opposition you are facing, it is necessary to deal with these positively, and to work with the unconscious patterns that are holding you back.**

This is of course a multilayered situation that requires ongoing healing. Yet while it is not always necessary to "name every demon," it is necessary to understand that much contributes to this situation that sits in the energy field and subconscious of the person dealing with an addiction, often undetected over many lifetimes.

As we note elsewhere, energy clearings can free one of current and past life trauma, entities, energy forms, ancestral patterns and trauma, cultural matrixes, and other energy traps that can ensnare one as fully as any deeply embedded physical drive for food or other chemicals.

We would say, that in your case, dear one, you are highly motivated to improve your life and move to a new and higher level—a higher form of self-awareness, growth, and healing. We do not agree that you are "sinking lower" into food addiction, as you have declared energetically in your statements to us that you are determined to better your life on all levels, including this one.

Though it is not necessary to name every form of opposition you are facing, it is necessary to deal with these positively, and to work with the unconscious patterns that are holding you back. Some of this can be addressed with tapping (Emotional Freedom Technique). We would tap not only to release the extra weight and the addictions, but to reassure your child self that she is safe now. That there is no need for her to carry extra weight through you, or to use eating as an emotional buffer zone between her and the world.

There are many helpful websites and books on Tapping, and plentiful videos on YouTube.com that support those wishing to release the subconscious blocks holding them back (in relationships, food and eating, financial abundance, and other areas). As you tap lightly on the meridian points of face and upper body, you touch upon the unconscious influences holding a negative pattern in place, opening it up gently, so it can be revised to a much higher vibrational pattern. This is a very simple, painless way to shift unconscious fears and blockages.

We would move beyond what is called "behavior modification" and leave all thoughts of "diets" to one side, though it is important to avoid those processed foods that you (and millions of others) are addicted to, that drive you to eat more of those and similar foods. These food products have been chemically treated and processed to do exactly that—to addict you to them. Most commercially sold cookies, crackers, breads, cereals, soft drinks, pastas, canned foods, and even whole frozen meals, for instance, contain chemicals created to achieve this—the constant buying and eating of food.

Carbohydrates and refined sugars not only raise your blood sugar in ways that require you to fulfill the need to lift it again an hour or two later. They also slow or stop any kind of release of body fat, and induce cravings and feelings of "need" that are not a need, but a chemically induced craving.

We would create a daily diet—not a weight loss diet, but an everyday one—that consists of 90% fresh, organic, raw fruits, vegetables, and unprocessed legumes, eaten with brown rice, quinoa and similar healthful choices. Release all meat and dairy products, as these are also highly processed, highly contaminated substances. We would drink the 8 to 10 glasses of water a day recommended by nutritionists. And we encourage everyone to get a structured water filter, as structured water will purify and enliven your entire system, and lift it (including your etheric body) to a higher level vibrationally.

Think of yourself as someone who lives off of water—that being the main ingredient to your physical health, besides proper rest and relaxation, exercise you enjoy, moderate sunlight, fresh air, daily meditation time, and spending time in Nature.

We would begin doing this purely to feel better in your body, to be kind to yourself, as forms of self-Love and self-nurturing, and not because you are punishing yourself for being "bad" or releasing old habits out of self-criticism.

All of this requires a spiritual commitment as much as a mental and physical one. Once you acclimate to cleaner, higher eating, you will wonder how you ever ate as much or as often as you did, and why you fell prey to the advertising, the false promises of foods and drinks that are masquerading as "quick" or "low-calorie" when they carry their own dangers that are worse than the higher calorie choices.

If you are able to fast healthfully, taking only water and/or fresh vegetable broth for several days at a time, this can purify and reset your system to a far higher level, making it easier to institute changes as you return to eating fresh organic foods. You will need to follow a specific fasting protocol, and check first with a health practitioner to make sure that a fast will not harm or throw off your system in any way. Everyone's physical condition is unique.

In this new life, in addition to seeing your therapist and doing tapping each day, you will also be doing energy clearings—pick one at a time, and do it several times a week till you are ready to move on to the next, or to do a live session with a capable practitioner.

Some excellent recorded clearings can be found online that are empowered with higher energies and the assistance of many higher beings who are able to cleanse your energies without a shock to your system. They will be moving entities, stuck energies, old trauma (current life, ancestral, cultural, and past life), and other impediments out of your system, cleansing you of presences that are keeping you in unconscious patterns that are not for your higher good.

Your Spirit team (and we encourage you to speak with them each morning, and any time during the day) are telling us that this is not a purely physical problem, in which you are simply addicted to food on a physical level. Yes, that is there, and there are foods you must stop eating in order to release the addiction cycle fully. Yet they are saying that 90 percent of the issue is etheric, mental, and emotional.

You are well capable of working this through, dear one. In therapy you will work out the current, closer-to-the-surface issues that come up as you uncover old pain and past situations that may have contributed to the need to protect yourself with the feeling of fullness, and carrying more weight than you need.

A spiritually aware therapist will also understand that Light Bringers are highly empathic, and that this carries its own complications. Many empaths overeat, because in doing so, they no longer have to feel so much, so often—it dulls their emotional responses and inner senses.

They easily move in and out of their bodies, according to whether they feel safe being there or not. For many, food is a way to ground themselves in their bodies, to distract from emotional conflict, and to create an emotional buffer zone between them and their own energies and emotions, not to mention that of their family, co-workers, and community. Empaths are in constant "energy reading" mode, ongoing and mainly unconscious.

# It is not unusual for people to draw to a Lightworker for reasons they are not consciously aware of.

This ongoing receiving of energy can extend to ancestors, childhood friends, and those you still have old soul contracts with, including old lovers, friends, children, and spouses from this and other lives. The energetic messaging can also come from old bosses, co-workers, neighbors—people you knew months or years ago and have no intention of outwardly contacting ever again. Yet the etheric ties remain.

It is not unusual for people to draw to a Lightworker for reasons they are not consciously aware of. Many are unconsciously asking for help, healing, understanding, or just Love and acceptance. Your Light is noted by everyone, and many will respond with a neediness energy that can be overwhelming or taxing to filter out.

To complicate matters further, most Lightworkers do not have the clear etheric and interpersonal boundaries in place to assist them in ensuring that others do not leech off of their energies, cling to them emotionally, or move into their energy field to bask in that Light, thereby adding to the weight that the empath is already carrying.

Most Light Beings in human form are kind and compassionate, and cannot bear to see another suffer. And so, yes—they will develop habits such as overeating or compulsive eating or other compulsions and defenses, to create a barrier between them and the internal stress they feel nearly all the time, as they try to heal the world.

All of this must be realized, dear one. Yet your story is not unusual, and you are moving forward all the time.

You have been creating personal boundaries that will not tolerate bad behavior from a partner, spouse, or anyone. You have been creating a new life in which you care for and honor yourself and your life purpose. And you have decided that you want body and mind, as well as spirit and energies, to be healthy, balanced, and free of toxins and dense attachments.

Rather than calling the food addiction a disease, we would say, it is an insufficient barrier between you and what you have suffered, and what you experience each day as a sensitive intuitive.

Your natural inclination is to live in a place of Peace and unity, not a divisive place of conflict and sorrow. Seeing, from childhood, the shadows and density of the planet you had come to, and the ill treatment you suffered, you early on decided to find ways to seek comfort and refuge from the onslaught of the energies of confusion and sadness.

**You are the only one to declare yourself innocent, sacred, and holy, and to end the blame, the self-criticism, and the shame-based beliefs that you are not worthy of complete health.**

And so now you are beginning to realize that that refuge is within you, tapped into via meditation or time in Nature, high vibrational music or creative pursuits, or all of that and more. You are at a place now where you must create a quiet place within yourself to return at any time. You must daily decide that you will receive both the higher wisdom needed for you to live a fulfilling life—your higher self's vision for you, while building energetic boundaries between you and that which is not for your higher good.

Your refuge will not be found in substances that alter your emotional frequency and brain activity, such as food will do. And with millions of other Lightworkers, you are also coming to depend less and less on solid food. Over time, your body and emotions would be troubled by the heaviness of the old diet, and wonder why you are trying to reinvest in a lost system.

We are flowing energies to you and to all who wish to be assisted in this area. For you are not moving backwards but forwards now. You are the only one to determine your complete safety inwardly and outwardly. The only one to construct those boundaries, including not allowing the brainwashing and systematic chemical and energetic entrainment of any culture or system to determine your choices.

You are the only one to declare yourself innocent, sacred, and holy, and to end the blame, the self-criticism, the accusations, and the shame-based beliefs that you are not worthy of complete health, complete wholeness.

For you were made for nothing else, as God/Goddess in human form, anchoring Light for Lady Gaia and all of humanity. That is plenty, and it is always enough.

# 14

# On Grief, and Feeling Lost on the Path

*I was feeling so much love and joy, and imagined being part of the Ascension process. I have been able to see things since I was a child, and have had many strange experiences, including meeting an Arcturian in an astral travel experience.*

*I have had a very hard life with abuse, and sacrificed a lot for my younger siblings—I raised them. Last September, my younger sister died. She just died in her sleep, and there is no concrete reason for it. It seems as if she just wanted to leave her body, and did that, and did not come back to it.*

*She died alone, and I feel responsible, because I could have done more for her, but we had begun to push each other away.*

*Her death has me full of negative emotions. I don't care about anything anymore. I don't believe in Ascension or anything anymore. I kind of hate the Angels, and feel very used and abused, and I feel these things for my sister as well. I don't want to have kids anymore. I can't see pictures of kids or be around them. I kind of hate them. I started to think about having an affair, and have been shoplifting. All these things to feel better. I don't care about consequences.*

*I still see the Angel lights (flashes or streaks of bright light) sometimes. They remind me that they are here, but who cares if they are. They are useless. We live in a 3D reality, and it sucks. I don't believe we will go higher and be free, or be more than this. I would love to be able to transition into being nonphysical, and be able to fly wherever I wanted, and manifest whatever I wanted. This is not possible, and I have lost all faith or hope it will ever happen.*

*I now feel angry with the spiritual community and their lack of groundedness. I see them as delusional, as dreamers, or people who need a wake-up call.*

*I don't like the advice I have been given by psychics (I consulted many after my sister died, and everything they said has now been revealed to be wrong). These people who say they can channel, really just say a lot of b.s., and they really don't care if you're hurting. Human emotion and connection are really lacking within the spiritual groups I have communicated with. They make a show of caring, but when something happens, they don't really care and aren't there for you.*

*Is this pain and hate part of the process too? I'm not sure what is happening to me, and if I'll ever find joy again, or return to a spiritual path again. It feels to me that I am off it, even though I was told by psychics that I am part of the Ascension process, part of the second wave, and that I would start hearing my sister and be able to channel her. I have been told so*

*many times that I can channel, but so far I think all
that they said was wrong.*

*My sister was able to channel, she said, and it
seemed so. She also communicated with animals, but
was also suffering so much, emotionally. Now she is
no more. Being in a different form is no comfort, it
means that the girl does not exist anymore.*

*I don't understand the point of being born to suffer
and then die, and never feel joy while alive, and then
to change form. I wish she had never been born, then
I would know her only as her true self who is on the
Other Side, and not have to suffer so much for the girl
that was here.*

*I wish that I was never born, and that everyone was
never born. Humans are parasites, and I don't think
we have a purpose. We are someone's experiment and
being used, and we aren't helping Gaia. She would be
better off if humans had never populated or evolved
on this planet.*

*Those are my feelings. I am looking for a little bit of
hope, so somehow someone can make me feel better.
I'm a fallen Angel in a way, and wondering if I can
be saved. I really don't have much hope that I will be,
and that anything really exists or matters in the end.*

*What do you have to say for the people who were
on the path of Ascension, and then got knocked down
and have completely fallen?*

*I know I have written a lot of harsh things here. I
just wanted to be completely honest, no matter how
bad it makes me look or sound, and I know it's bad.
I appreciate honesty and bluntness, but also please
remember that I lost my baby girl who never found
happiness, and that is not something you get over.*

You stand in the fire, dear one, and despite all its powerful,
transmuting qualities, it is still a painfully difficult, even a
frightening place to be.

You still desire the higher dimensions—the freedom that a higher density being experiences all the time, being able to transport themselves, and to manifest outwardly in an instant. You have for the moment chosen a lack of belief in any life after the physical. You are despising physical death due to the fact that transition into nonphysical does not appear as you would prefer.

Almost no one living in what is still in many ways a third dimensional Earth, ever wants to experience losing a loved one to physical death. You have witnessed your sister's transition as the disappearance of someone you loved, raised, and protected. And to not know where her precious and loving presence has gone to, nor be able to connect with her, is making your experience of loss all the more difficult.

You are not so much in hatred as in shock, dear one. You are not so much in disbelief of Life after Life, as understanding the finality and utterly temporary nature of the physical in a whole new way. You are in fact traveling out of the physical, in the sense that you now see well beyond it. This could not have occurred on such a profound level without your experiencing releasing one you have loved from this experience, as she travels back Home, from a place of low density to her natural place of very high, refined energies. So refined that you cannot see her from where you are now, and certainly, cannot sense her inwardly, amidst the rage and shock of your grief.

Though you say you no longer feel connected to the Angels, and no longer believe or care about spiritual matters, you do in fact care more deeply about them now than you ever have.

This is why you are refusing all expressions of false spirituality. It has led you to demand only honesty from now on, on every level of life. It makes the shoplifting and the thought of an affair easier and even seem sensible, since all rules are broken, now that the greatest one has been broken.

The veil has fallen from your eyes. You no longer live in any form of illusion or pretense, of promises or "belief systems." Life must prove itself to you now, including life beyond what you have known as a human in physical form.

And yet, this is where you have wanted to be. For all its discomfort, this is the path you chose before incarnating, and your sister was fully in agreement with that plan. With her seemingly too-early departure from the physical, she knew she would help you reach the understanding and evolvement that she herself had already reached.

Do not mistake this journey you are on and the life you have lived for Who you really are, and what you have come to experience and to gain. You are correct when you say that your sister actually belongs not to this Earth but to the higher etheric world of energy, Light, pure Love, and joyful expression of the true self. She belongs to other, higher dimensional realms— higher density planets and star systems. And she lived out a far higher life purpose than what you could see.

### When you speak of flying here or there, or manifesting instantly, you speak of what you witness in your sister's own experience and your own, as you travel in the higher realms.

Your sister (who has also in other lives been your daughter, your friend, your comrade) is a brilliant Light Being, aware of energy on a very high level, able to interpret, read, communicate not only with people and animals but life and energy forms of all kinds. She travels this Universe with great facility and Joy, not to establish any kind of permanence or safety as humans try to design for themselves right from the start, but for the pure Experience of Knowing and Understanding, for the increasing wisdom of serving others in ways that will serve not only their higher good, but the higher good of the collective consciousness, and of all life.

On Earth she was a Healer, a Communicator, and an Interpreter who could bring through not only messages from the higher realms, but the very high frequencies embedded in them that would not only restore a person's sense of higher self, but aid them in remembering their higher purpose, connecting them to energies that would assist them in tapping into the resources needed to complete their purpose.

This is a rare gift. At one point in her timeline, your beloved realized on a higher level that her work would be far better accomplished were she to return to the nonphysical. This would enable her energies to reach a greater number of people, animals, plant life—all of Earth life as it increases in vibration.

And so when you speak of flying here or there, or manifesting instantly—you speak of what you witness in your sister's experience and your own, as you travel in the higher realms.

This comes from the deeply held memories you carry forward into the day, from your sleep state. You visit her often in your etheric body, while your physical body rests at night. During that time, she is explaining, in her own way (via energy transmission) why she decided to leave when she did, and how that decision weaves into your own evolvement. She is aware of how shocking and painful her leaving was to you. She asks now that you trust and honor her path, wherever it takes her.

The Earth notion of death is mired in many thousands of years of mental programming. That and the much-reduced human capacity for a fully conscious visiting of the higher realms keeps anyone's understanding of Life after Life very small. Increasingly, many are overcoming this as empowering energies reach the Earth from your sun, via the Great Central Sun.

And so your idea of death is to fixate on the loss of a person's physical presence, as proof that they are no more. And that you have lost, and are irretrievably given over to suffering now. In a sense, your suffering is only as deep as your Love for this dear and brilliant higher being, and is entirely understandable. It is a way of honoring her life. But it is not where she herself desires for you to live for any extended period of time.

You have given her many months of your sadness, and she understands your feeling that her departure was unnecessary and could have been avoided. She understands that it seems she gave up amidst the pain and challenges of her Earth life. She knows you feel that you should have been there when it happened, or made life easier for her, so that she would not have had to leave so suddenly, and seemingly for no other reason than her suffering.

We assure you, she knew her suffering, but she was not in a state of giving up and feeling it was useless to go on. She had learned what she came here to learn, and was ready to move on to continue her work on a higher level. Believe us when we say that many millions all over the world are doing that exact same thing, despite the shock and upset that their loved ones are left in.

Your sister wishes you to know that All Is Well. That your emotional state, though understandable and full of compassion and Love for her, is not what she would prefer for you, and not what you prefer for yourself, though you do not consciously accept that yet. She is Home where she longed to be in this last Earth life, and in all Earth lives she has ever lived, being a highly refined being with many Angelic aspects, and an Angelic Love of higher dimensional music, Nature, animals, children, and all natural forms of life.

## You are surrounded by Angels at every moment, but they are not here to ensure that you have a life that is different from what you planned.

Her leaving does not mean that you did not do enough, or that you were not there for her at the right time. She would not have left the Earth in front of you, as the shock of that moment would have only deepened the grief you feel now. Be aware that no one leaves by accident, even when they leave a bit earlier than originally planned (which was not the case with your sister). That leaving is interwoven into the higher path of their soul growth. This is why she is saying, "All Is Well."

She is not out of kilter or thrown into shock by her departure, even though you are.

She is also asking us to relay that you have her same gifts. That you are of the same soul family, with the same soul mission, even though your individual paths of soul growth differ somewhat. And that she has not abandoned you!—she is being emphatic on that point—and wishes you to release all feelings of abandonment and loss.

You are surrounded by Angels at every moment, but they are not here to ensure that you have a life that is different from what you planned before arriving in this Earth life. You were clear that you were not coming into yet another Earth life for an easygoing, painless time, or even an only slightly challenging one.

They are here to ensure that you *remain* on that path, and draw the highest and finest forms of Wisdom and Understanding from it. There are forms of Knowing and evolvement that would not have been available to you without another Earth life experience, particularly at this crucial time. You came here for that, in addition to experiencing your own Ascension (which is still ongoing) and to assist in Earth's Ascension.

Those who explain that your sister is not gone, but simply in another form, are correct in their description, even if it feels to you to be an "easy out" or a weak revision of the word "loss." In fact, you have not lost. Though your sister has completed her transition back into the etheric, she is around you far more than you know. You visit her in the etheric in your sleep state, and she visits you in your physical life, both day and night, as she is capable of multilocating in different dimensions in a conscious and immediate way.

You are despising physical existence because it feels too separate from what you consider to be a spiritual one. And so the spiritual becomes unthinkable, because you feel denied and betrayed by it. It is in fact, physical existence that betrays the etheric. Life on Earth has for thousands of years stepped away from connection to the etheric by the systematic lowering of Earth consciousness.

That has ended now, though at present, the old cycles familiar to Earth beings are still being played out, in the last round of the game. This does not mean that things are not changing drastically. Ascension means that you will be able to connect with and hear and eventually even see those who are visiting you in their Lightbody or etheric form.

This does not mean that Ascension isn't happening. It only means that Earth's Ascension has not yet developed to where you feel it's moving forward to a higher level of living. This is particularly difficult when you see everything through the fog of grief.

**One day in an unexpected moment, you will release enough of the grief and anger to see through that last veil.**

Your sister also wishes you to know that you are using your gifts powerfully and brilliantly in the etheric—as your higher self and soul, and as you travel at night in your sleep state. You do not have to feel good about life, or feel "spiritual" as in feeling the presence of higher beings around you. You don't have to like the Angels. You don't have to feel filled with the Joy and higher Light of the higher dimensions. Nothing of the sort.

If you wish to cry or rage or stay separate from the life around you (or rebel against the old norms), you may do so. Yet she is saying, This is temporary, and not Who you really are.

One day in an unexpected moment, you will release enough of the grief and anger to see through that last veil, which claims that "there is nothing beyond this," and that once a loved one is lost as far as physical Earth life is concerned, they are lost to everything. Deep down, you know that cannot be true, as you have memories of your sister in the higher realms and in other Earth lives—this is one reason why this Earth life has been so painful to you.

*Did I love and protect her enough?* you are asking. *Did I do all I could? Surely not, if she died so young, and before me, her older sibling.*

These are questions that plague so many in their grief. You assist both yourself and her by allowing your sister her path, as she has allowed you yours. Though your grief is difficult for her to witness, she knows it does not fully define you, even if it has revised your outlook in significant ways.

*For no one can lie to you now, dear one, least of all yourself.* You have released the vestiges of the old, third dimensional Earth life. You speak of having "completely fallen," and yet, this has been the beginning of your complete awakening.

All is coming into the Light, and all is revealing itself in perfect time and way.

This is the Ascension you feel to have left behind. And yet—you have now begun it more fully, and one day, will experience it more joyfully than you could have ever dreamt of.

Speak to your loved one whenever you wish—she will hear you—even if it is only to express your shock and outrage that she would leave you as and when she did. Allow her spirit to be present with you. You have not lost her. You have only lost an appearance (and you have come to distrust those).

You have not lost that which shall always remain.

Yes, the release of the physical by a loved one can feel to be an impossible weight to carry. And so put it down, dear one. If you cannot put it into the hands of your soul or higher self, give it to the Earth. Give it to us.

Honor your beloved's choices and life path. And honor your own path! For this you came.

# 15

# On Creating Your Life Work and Independent Forms of Service

*Why, every time I think I have a grasp on my purpose, mission, and message, and I start exploring it, investing significant time and energy into it (e.g., a new business setup)—why, after I've put so much effort into its creation, do I lose my connection to it?*

*It no longer excites or attracts me, let alone inspires or motivates. I get great responses from others to the idea itself and its value, so it has merit, yet after a time, I totally disconnect.*

*I believe I know the core of my purpose: I'm a messenger, a sharer of information/knowledge and aspiring role model for our new 5D paradigm. But I simply can't get a handle on what the information is I'm here to share, and to whom.*

*My challenge is, How do I do that in a way that resonates and inspires me past the initial stages, and then be able to identify my real "tribe"?*

*Knowing we have a role and a message to share, yet not understanding what it is specifically we're here to express, and to whom, feels frustrating at a time when it feels like there is an increasingly urgent need for us all to step up and live our life missions.*

*Is it simply about timing?*

*I assume it may also be about moving beyond ego and identity, and allowing a new being-ness to emerge as we move into our multidimensional selves.*

*If so, how do we express ourselves authentically in the interim, without a label to describe what we do? And how do we earn a living offering our own services, if we don't have the clarity needed to share those services?*

*And how do we live from our new, emerging 5D consciousness in the existing 3D world of "work"? It feels like there is a magnetic repulsion when exploring how to apply skills within the paradigm that is still essential for "earning" a living.*

*From my perspective, 3D companies do not feel as if they are compromising themselves by functioning between 3D and 5D. When I've undertaken even simple customer service roles, my presence soothes colleagues and customers, yet ruffles those in more senior management roles, as I find myself constantly seeking new ways to deliver better service.*

*As a change agent, it's impossible not to want to improve existing systems—diplomatically—but it's never well-received.*

*Organizations seem to recognize the misalignment or disparity in energies when you apply to work with them, closing off the opportunity at the outset. At least, that's been my experience, where there's an excellent skills match.*

*Is there any chance of any external negative influences (entities, attachments, implants, etc.) affecting our progress?*

*If so, how do we know what are our own issues to resolve, and what other factors may be impeding our progress? How do we counteract them?*

*Is it simply about ensuring our vibration/ frequencies are consistently at their highest level, or do we need external assistance to identify and remove whatever may be affecting us?*

W e will address your questions one by one.

You speak of having a desire to create something born of inspiration—ideas that others relate to positively, and that you have initial excitement about. You have found that you then lose that initial excitement and motivation, and release the idea before it comes to fruition.

This is not unusual. When an idea is new, it has a shine to it that can easily fade. Some say, in fact, that as soon as you think of a thing, it quickly becomes "old." You must leave that initial time of inspiration to fully set it in motion.

As you step beyond your initial vision and start fleshing out your idea, the everyday ins and outs—the practical matters of websites and budgets and marketing to your tribe—crowd in to where things no longer feel to be part of the higher realms, but mired in the old third dimension. Though Earth is moving steadily into the fifth dimension, life here still carries many of the old realities and vibrations, plus the Ascension pressures and demands of transformation and release of the old.

You are growing and evolving at such a rate that any specific advice we could offer would very quickly fade in the Light of Who you are now becoming. But we will offer a few ideas, which are something you can consider and draw solutions from.

First, offer whatever you can offer, right now. Today.

## Get into the habit now of finding what makes you most joyful in terms of giving to others, and start doing that in some small way.

Offer something small enough that you don't feel you are "betting the ranch" on its fulfillment. You are simply, for example, posting something on social media each day that inspires and encourages a particular group of people. This might be the elderly, working mothers, those with disabilities, those seeking spiritual comfort and encouragement, those healing from compulsive behaviors or addictions—the list is endless!

Whom do you feel drawn to help? Whom do you imagine yourself serving, in beautiful, fulfilling ways?

Get into the habit now of finding what makes you most joyful in terms of giving to others, and start doing that in some small way that doesn't feel to be a big production. Create a way to give that doesn't feel as big as sending an email to 10,000 people, or writing a book, or putting services and products out into the world that haven't been tried and tested yet. Taking big steps all at once can leave you sitting and wondering whether any of it will go over well, or even be noticed.

This is part of what you are facing, and so (like many), you then begin to disconnect from the original idea. You're thinking, "Now it's real," and realizing that you are exposing this wonderful, visionary inner self to the reality of other people's opinions. That can be intimidating, particularly if you have not yet identified your tribe—the particular group of people you are serving. It has put off more than a few Light Bringers from their true path, as they doubt the things they have to offer.

Yet it is not so much that you do not believe in yourself. It's more a question of, "Is it wise of me to gamble my self-belief in a public way? To open myself up to being criticized, or worse, ignored?"

That can be a frightening prospect. One that many people go out of their way to avoid.

We would say that though only a minority of people in most cultures are completely self-employed, it is actually the majority who would immensely benefit from and greatly enjoy being self-employed. Particularly if they could, for example, take time off when needed, spend only five or six hours a day at work, or work only three or four days a week, instead of the usual 40 hours or more.

And if they could do what they truly believed in and loved doing, even if some of the time they were caught up in administrative, marketing, or accounting chores.

They would still vote in favor of their independence, if they fully believed they could withstand the possibility that their work wouldn't be received well enough to earn them what they require for living and saving. The idea, whatever it is, for their product or service would have to interest them and other people long enough and fully enough for them to create something lasting and income-producing.

That hesitance, and that inner reserve, is natural and understandable. But it cannot be the whole story.

You do not have these creative desires for the thrill of beginning them and not fulfilling them. They are there to be not only born but lived out. The question is, Can you allow that? Can you birth something and give it the time needed to find its legs, and learn to walk?

Can you extend the kind of patience and self-Love needed to learn how to run your own show, and to do it with confidence and the skills required to make it not only lasting (though reincarnating from time to time), but an Abundant channel of income? (If that is what you envision.)

We would say, you most assuredly have those skills. But you are allowing your subconscious to run you, letting old fears and family and ancestral ties, patterns, and influences warn you not to go into business for yourself, as it is "too chancy." Most men have been strictly trained, for example, to "provide a steady income" for their family, and to feel to be a failure if they are not able to do so. Many women are strictly trained to believe that "Women aren't as financially well off if they're single," or that "Women aren't as successful at running businesses as men are," whether these beliefs are stated out loud, or simply inside the energetic makeup of that person's upbringing.

Whether fears and warnings such as this (and there are many different ones) come from family, education, culture, or something in your DNA, they are there, and need to be faced and dealt with.

The left brain can also be unsupportive in its own way. It will believe it is protecting you by holding you back, saying things such as, "This is too much work! What if no one cares? Let's forget about this. Nice idea, but not the right time for it . . . "

Yet you can face down this opposition, with focus and clear intent, and by rewriting subconscious fears. You say you know the core of your purpose, and that is fine. Now concentrate on the skills you love to use, to express that purpose.

We also always recommend to Light Bringers who are beginning a new venture that they have some form of financial support, whether a proven form of independent work or a day job, to use as income as they are developing their new work.

This takes the pressure off the new area, until you can begin to create sufficient income from it. Possibly, you will never care about making money from it, and that is fine. Yet if you are wishing to create financial income from a new venture, you will need a clear idea of what you are offering to people, a clear idea of who it is you are speaking to (choose a specific group, and one you know how to speak to), and a good website—there are many excellent examples to follow, in every field of work.

Also read up on solid, proven marketing advice, which is certainly available in numerous programs, books, and videos.

## To serve any one group of people or individuals effectively, first ask what they most need.

There are no "success secrets" being hidden from you. The obstacles you are facing are internal ones. Yet those can be the hardest ones for anyone to realize, for you are so used to them, you hardly know they are there. This is where energy clearings come in, performed by an experienced and effective shaman or energy worker (in person or via live or recorded video). You may not know what is blocking you, but you will know the nature of it, by the obstacles you are facing within your own thoughts and feelings.

Finding your tribe—those people you most want to assist—is powerfully important. You must determine this before moving forward. If you wish to serve, you must do more than simply express your own favorite ideas. Speak with your Spirit team, and require them to direct you inwardly—with words, or with outer signs, inner nudges, or an energy download that brings the answer forward in any number of ways, including infusing your own thoughts with their higher ideas and solutions, so that you know both who you want to help, and how.

Once you have a clear idea of this—the higher solutions will light up for you, and feel right inwardly, when they come in— you then need to find out what that particular tribe needs most, in the area you can serve them in.

You can ask, in conversation, on social media, or in a group email, "What troubles you most about _____?" or "What is your biggest question about how to _____?" or something along those lines. Let people answer and *tell you what it is that they need.*

This is crucial. To serve any one group of people or individuals effectively, first ask what they most need, keeping in mind your particular skills and resources.

Your new work identity, if you wish to call it that, will not come from a 3D perspective. It will come from a 5D perspective, and will be heart-centered, not left-brain survival-based or scarcity-oriented. You may or may not have a name or label as you begin. It might only be a descriptive phrase of how you want to help others, and that is fine. Many of the third dimensional labels are falling by the wayside now. They no longer suit the Light Beings, the *homo lumens* that human beings are becoming.

Yes, timing can be an issue. We would say, that if you are feeling a need to help others, and are already attempting to build the structure by which to do that, the time is here. But do so in steps, not great leaps that intimidate the ego-mind and freeze you into inactivity just as you're getting started.

You are most assuredly moving *beyond* the ego-mind, and moving into the heart-mind. That must be central to whatever you envision or build now, or that work will quickly become irrelevant in these new, higher energies reaching the Earth and shifting human life and consciousness at Lightspeed.

It is difficult to earn an independent living in any area without first having clarity about what you are doing. You most definitely need clarity regarding what it is you are offering people. This saves you from overgiving and overdelivering to an unhealthy extent. It also saves you from feeling you haven't fully given on any one level, because you have been working to offer too much in a very general way.

If you are working in what many Lightworkers call "a 3D job," you must remember that though you have a mission to fulfill, not everyone around you will be in synch with those energies. It is fine to want to contribute to wherever you are working. But keep in mind that these may well be people who are on an entirely different path from your own. They will not understand much of your progressive energy, let alone your words, actions, and motivations.

Recall your own slower understanding before you came to the place you are in now. Have compassion for those who are on a different path of evolvement. Do not ask them to grasp or even be aware of energies and realizations they are not ready for. You would not ask a seven-year-old to do college-level chemistry experiments, for example.

So you will not be applying 5D skills per se, in a 3D environment, except for the 5D skill of loving and accepting yourself and all others, as you anchor higher Light wherever you are. You will need to "come out of your head" while at work, and relate to others (whether coworkers, bosses, clients, or customers) as people whom you can serve in positive ways. Release the idea that they are judging or excluding you because your energies do not match theirs. When you release the need to judge others, and to judge what are termed "3D environments," others often release their judgments of you.

Now, this is not to say that there are no uncomfortable moments, for even the most loving and kindest Lightworker. There can be many. And so, as you are being clear with the Universe on what you want to create, you might want to use the

"Working With Energy" recorded meditation and manifestation tool, to work with the energy of a situation you want to create, such as a new job or business. You do this before you know how it will manifest, and what outer form it will take.

You might also want to use affirmations, or to daily spend time visualizing yourself working happily in the perfect work environment for you, until that situation materializes outwardly for you.

These are just a few ideas. We would do energy work in meditation, using affirmations, visualizations, and positive expectation, before making assumptions about what any one workplace or job might be like.

Something that empaths tend to do, is to brace themselves for a rough ride, when looking for work or going into a job every day. They have spent decades feeling other people's pains, anger, grief, and loneliness. They have absorbed emotions, ideas, and life philosophies, working hard energetically on a subconscious level to heal their families, their whole ancestral line, their neighbors, lovers, spouses, friends, coworkers—only to see that these people find that "help" to be intrusive or judgmental at least half the time. They may also see these people develop a dependency on their empathic, intuitive friend or family member, which is draining and weighty for the empath to carry on a daily basis.

We would suggest that you take the far healthier, lighter path. Release the need to fix every job and workplace, help every coworker, and generally "make the world a better place" in situations that have no any interest in that growth.

## Release the need to advance every place you work in. Your energies are already anchoring beautiful levels of Light in that atmosphere.

It is not that your assistance is not needed. Most assuredly it is, and everyone can be thankful for it. But you cannot solve another's problems for them, and cannot learn their wisdom and understanding for them, which they came here to learn and absorb for themselves, even if you feel that might lighten the load on the energies you carry or pick up on intuitively.

Loving someone—individuals, groups, work environments, the world—is often a matter of letting go and releasing them to their own higher path. What others believe, what they think of you, and where they are going in life is truly no one's business but their own. And so, release the need to advance every place you work in. Your energies are already anchoring beautiful levels of Light in that atmosphere, dear one! You are doing a great deal, just by being there.

What other human beings and even whole organizations need, is for someone to believe in them. To see their higher Light, and to speak to that, not the lower ego-mind, the survival-based personality. Just by loving and accepting someone and expecting only the best from them, you solve the majority of problems that come from being a sensitive person. Many will unconsciously brace themselves for refusal or rejection on some level, because they know those around them just don't "get it" yet.

And so, put down that great sense of mission. It is already fulfilled, the moment you allow yourself to love yourself and others, as you all are right now. If you wish to improve existing systems, do so in small ways that no one will much notice, let alone object to.

Fill every moment on the job with higher Light—send a ray of Light from your heart to all you encounter, from the least-lauded employee to the biggest executive. Affirm lightly, "Only Divine Will is done here," and then let go!

What greater act is there, than to love others, and to bless them with their higher good? And to seek to serve their higher good, as well as your own?

Often, what is happening when an evolved person is interviewing for a job, and is quickly excluded from any chance of employment, is that the person doing the interviewing feels a bit intimidated by them. This can come partly from silent judgments the interviewee may have regarding how that organization is run, and partly from their own progressive energies and nature.

Again, send a ray of Light from your heart to the interviewers, and to all who will be deciding whether to hire you. At this point, you have written down and affirmed aloud or in writing, many times, the job you want—the work atmosphere, hours, boss, pay, coworkers, skills you want to use, and the kind of fulfillment you wish to gain from it.

You have then not given way to despair or the judgment of "3D work environments." Instead, you have specifically affirmed that you are now finding the role and environment that you will enjoy and appreciate, and that affirms your energies, presence, and abilities.

This too is serving, and is one reason why Milton wrote, "They also serve who stand and wait," in his Sonnet 19. Read that sonnet when you have a moment, as it comments in its own way that all the outer action in the world is not necessarily "needed" by the Universe.

Your own "mild yoke" is learning to love yourself as well as others, without judgment.

It would be difficult to ensure that your energies are constantly humming at the highest level when (as with most human beings) they don't reach that frequency very often. Yet those high vibrational moments can occur during moments quietly spent in Nature, in an expression of Love to a loved one, in an act of giving to another, in meditation, in times of creative expression, when immersed in high vibrational music, or during similar high vibrational moments.

It would take a powerful leap into enlightenment to achieve that vibration as a new norm, and though that can and does occur, it is not how most people reach it. This is why we strongly recommend spending quiet time each day, quieting your thoughts, speaking with your Spirit team to ask what you need to know right now, spending quiet time in Nature, following a guided meditation, or listening to a live or recorded energy clearing.

All of this brings you into closer vibration to your higher self, which is Who you are becoming.

You will not know all of your issues, for most are buried in your subconscious. Most assuredly, external help is often required to become clear of interferences and unwelcome presences, such as implants, entities, trauma, and old soul contracts, to name a few. This is why shamans and energy workers do the work they do, so avail yourself of every opportunity to work with someone who is honest, effective, and reliable in their work. Use your intuition and ask your team to lead you to the right energy workers for you. You are not alone in this, and need not feel that way.

In all, we would say that your first priority must not be to establish a business per se, but to establish an area of service to others. Begin that in small ways, before you expect it to become a solid channel of income. Develop it independently while earning your money elsewhere. When it becomes strong enough to support you financially, you will know—alert your Spirit team that they need to inform you of this, and listen for their answer.

Your work is in assisting humankind in their Ascension, in ways that most people can embrace and feel helped by.

It is all anyone can do, on this road to expressing Divine Love, and being Divine Love in human form.

# 16

# On Dealing with Past Life Trauma

*Certainly for me the Ascension process has been continual for the past year. Peculiar experiences are met with some sensible reasoning, but I am having a hard time wrapping my mind around the meaning or the reason for this:*

*One morning I woke up with much pain in my right shoulder and arm. I was glad it was massage day for me.*

*It is not uncommon for me to drift in and out of sleep during a session. So when that began to happen, I remained in a state of allowance. I have been getting regular massages for over 20 years, so this took me by surprise, as it was a first:* I experienced being in two places at once.

*I was totally present with the massage, because very painful electrical volts charged out of my right shoulder, back and side, down my arm and out my fingers. My right quarter was twitching and felt as though my right arm was unscrewing like a cap on a bottle.*

*All of a sudden, I was also in a prisoner of war camp, hanging by my wrists that had been bound with rope.*

*A Japanese man was torturing me with electric prods while screaming an unknown language at me. It was playing like a movie in my mind, happening in the now, yet I was also here in the now, receiving massage and releasing this terrible pain.*

*This felt like a past life regression (I have had several), except that I was also fully present here. I have been having glimpses since summer solstice of losing track of time. It can feel quite confusing, and I am ever grateful that my life allows me time to sort through this.*

*I am a 20-plus-year massage therapist, and have witnessed many people release old trauma attached to current physical pain on my table, but those traumas were from this life. I have read that we carry from life to life certain themes, so the experience makes sense, in that I have never in this life been able to hold my arms above my head for very long without pain.*

*During that experience I felt betrayed and sacrificed by the country I loved. In the past several years I have known other past life experiences of betrayal and sacrifice. My guides say this is my reminder to trust.*

*Learning to trust is huge for me and is something I rarely do. In this life trusting others (even my own family) has not turned out well, so I think perhaps the message from my guides is about trusting myself and my guides more.*

*Do you have insight to share on this?*

Your experience, though powerful, is not unusual. Millions are having similar experiences, though they are generally occurring in a person's dream state, when the personality and ego-mind will not fly into a panic and believe the body is multilocating, or that the mind is fracturing on some level.

The body work you received was merely a portal for your higher self to energetically bring up that which was crying out to be seen and healed.

You were indeed a captured soldier during World War II, and believed by the Japanese commanding officer at the time of your capture to be a foreign military spy. This was not the first life in which you were subjected to torture, imprisonment, or feelings of betrayal and abandonment, or sacrifice. You have belonged to other groups (spiritual, religious, community, political) in other lives that fell afoul of some local authority. You were punished in those lives for your beliefs or actions, or for what others mistook to be your beliefs, actions, or affiliations.

## Part of your life purpose in this Earth life is working with humanity to release the assumption that people naturally fall into categories.

In this life, with powerful and enlightening energies coming to Earth at increasing levels, all are being required to either Ascend or move onto another 3D timeline. As part of that process, you are releasing the shock and pain of these experiences, so that you can reap wisdom from them and move beyond them.

Your soul is seeking a healing from these disturbances. And your higher self is working with your Earth aspect to bring you to a consciousness where you are no longer directed by deep-seated feelings of abandonment, or of having been sacrificed to a captor's hatred, or a leader's failure to protect their people.

It is not, in fact, so much a feeling of having been abandoned or sacrificed, as a desire to no longer be defined purely by your role in a community—a cog in a wheel. Part of your life purpose in this Earth life is working with humanity to release and leave behind these assumptions that people naturally fall into categories and labels—and that those cultural affiliations and group beliefs define them.

This is a very old, very deep rut that human beings have felt safe in (or abandoned by) and defined by for millennia, and now that time is ending.

As you and others allow these images and feelings to come to the surface, you allow healing for the left-behind Earth self— all of the Earth lives in which you suffered jail time, torture, excommunication, death, or desertion due to human beliefs and authority structures.

As you heal these long-held tears in your spirit and psyche, you heal them in others as well. You unconsciously adjust and raise the frequency of their understanding of why human beings are on the Earth, and how they may serve their own and others' higher good.

## All is well, and all are safe, when all lay down their swords and shields.

You are in fact healing the very need for labels, categories, separatism, and ego identities. There is no need to hide, to rebel, or to defend when you are already sure of what you know. That quiet confidence and Peace of heart-mind are a potent source of inner power. They well outrun the need for outer justifications, identifications, and social groups to hide in.

All is well, and all are safe, when all lay down their swords and shields, and stop defending or attacking one belief system or another.

This and much more are your work on this beautiful planet, and you are bringing it forth perfectly. And so, do not expect all moments to make sense in the context of what you have experienced before now, for there has never been a "Now moment" quite like this one.

The Ascension of a planet from the lowest dimension to support human life into the next highest dimension (the fifth) is nothing less than a miracle. Yet the support and ongoing work of Light Bearers such as yourself make it an everyday occurrence, and a celebration of a freedom the Earth has not seen in millennia.

And so, allow these moments to come forward, and bless and release those old associations, memories, and pains. You may need to work with an experienced energy worker to work out of your system residual feelings of bitterness and loss, on both an etheric and a cellular level, and that is fine.

The path remains the same—you are remaking the old into the new, in new and beautifully higher ways.

# 17

# On Dealing with Disrespect from Others

*I don't know if anyone else is experiencing this, but a couple of friendships I've had for the last 7 years have become disrespectful.*

*One has turned into a lack of reciprocity, and the other, in the last eight months, has cancelled at least 80 percent of the time.*

*Are others experiencing disrespect, in any form, in their relationships in general?*

Most assuredly, many millions are seeing shifts in their relationships with friends, spouses, partners, fellow workers, and family members, in ways are shaking them up. They are either disappointed by these shifts or feeling that they need to release some persons from their lives, even those they never expected to let go of for any reason. This shift has been happening for a while now.

The powerful energetic move forward that began unveiling itself in December 2012 was not only one of astrological or metaphoric significance. From that time on, you began to fundamentally change who and what you are, and others did as well.

There is no going back now to how things were before. No returning to how you used to see the world, what you used to hold as true about yourself and others, or the reasoning you once used for doing the things you did. You are still in a period of accelerated change, and there is no way those changes would not affect your connections with others. Even those you used to trust, enjoy, lean on, and believe in wholeheartedly.

It is easy to feel let down or abandoned by someone after they change to a different view of life, and it becomes clear that you can no longer support who they are. Or perhaps, you are the one who has changed, and have come to realize that you can no longer connect with this person as you once did. In any event, one or both of you have changed, and there is no reconciling that.

These are natural signs of Ascension. They are the result of the kind of inner growth that is related to an increased connection to and awareness of Nature, of Earth's shifts, changes, and astrological alignments. And of your own shifting cellular and etheric makeup. They are not necessarily occurring because this person has become cold or unresponsive or uncaring, though it may look that way.

Perhaps they still do care. But your energy and theirs no longer flow together or meet and agree in midair as they once did. Keep in mind that with everyone you have been close to, there has been a telepathic and energetic connection, as well as an outer conversational one. You have been picking up on changes in your friends' lives, as they have been picking up on changes in yours. And often, if someone feels that their energies cannot flow easily and happily with yours, they will begin to release you, in ways they believe to be subtle and relatively pain-free. (And sometimes, in not-so-subtle ways.)

Your friend who has been canceling 80 percent of the time has effectively let go of you. And you must find a way to let go of them now, for there is little to nothing remaining of your connection. What you regard as a friendship is no longer in place, as you have both shifted so fully that the two people who were once friends are no more—two other people have come to take their place, and will only continue to evolve and shift over time.

## You are on a trajectory of accelerated growth that is best described as pure Transformation.

In fact, the evolvement that individuals and groups are seeing now is only speeding up. There is now no way for the post-2012 timeline to be considered an anomaly. The next five to six years will bring even greater changes in what human beings are capable of in spirit, mind, and body, and how they view their Earth, themselves, and one another.

You are on a trajectory of accelerated growth that is best described as pure Transformation. We spell it with a capital "T" because the importance of that term cannot be understated.

The friend who is not reciprocating your support or kindness is letting go in their own way. Allow others their shifts and evolvement, wherever that may take them, as you would desire them to allow you yours.

There are others whose growth, energetic vibration, and viewpoints are better attuned to your own than these dear ones who are now on a different path, a different trajectory, with a different purpose than your own.

It is easy to feel loss or regret for life changes such as these. And yet—they would not be occurring if you were not finally locating your true and authentic self, and being placed in situations that require you to release the old life so that the new one can come more fully into being.

And so we encourage all who are experiencing shifts in their connections with loved ones—sometimes, painful shifts that include shocks and feelings of betrayal or abandonment—to understand that your path, life purpose, and life presence are clarifying themselves more and more each day. There is now no stopping that particular cosmic vehicle you chose to ride so many eons ago, when you first thought of coming to the Earth plane and joining this Great Experiment in duality.

If you can now release the forms of duality that spawn judgment of yourself and others, you will do far better in this time of growth that is so sudden, so sped up, and so far-reaching, that some days it all feels more tumultuous than co-Creative and positive.

And yet—co-Creative is exactly what this time of expansion is. Allow these shifts, and release those who you feel are not honoring you, or no longer on your wavelength.

Expect to meet those who are far more on your (new and higher) frequency, dear one. For they seek you, just as you seek them.

Many are soul family members whose presence can bring you real Joy and recognition, and they look forward to knowing you on Earth as they do in the higher realms.

# 18

# On Dealing Positively with Illness and Disability

*Living in a body that has become prematurely (in my 3D opinion) incapacitated, of course I want my body to get well, yet it feels like this hibernation/ incubation is part of the journey.*

*My questions relate to the idea of, "How shall we then live?"*

*How do I respond to the feelings of grief over all the things I need to let go of (all the things I used to be able to do physically, cognitively, musically, etc.)?*

*How do I rest or grow into what Is?*

*How do I navigate the intersection between frustration and gratitude?*

This is an excellent and powerful question, and we are very glad you have asked it. You are both brave and open to Transformation (including healing), and that is why you have had the courage to take on this journey, and to ask these questions.

We would say, that you are completely correct when you say that your hibernation is a kind of incubation, and that it is part of your journey. Though it can be argued otherwise, even though you live on a tumultuous and often chaotic planet, there are no accidents.

Your Spirit team of guides, Angelic guardians, and higher self are assuring us that you did indeed plan to experience this current lack of mobility, and that this particular path you are on is enabling the energetic teachings and "downloads"—Light codes and inner vibrational shifts—that you are receiving at present.

We would not say that you will always be in this situation, for there are wheels quickly turning now, motivated by beautiful forms of higher intent, including powerful intervention by Galactic and etheric beings who are assisting your planet. These are uncovering forms of healing and renewal that have long been suppressed by the old power structure.

## The greatest movement you carved out for yourself to experience in this Earth life was the etheric one.

And so we would say, you may certainly grieve for what you feel you have lost. Yet the potential is strong for you to regain your mobility, in addition to your gaining what you are learning at present.

The cognitive functions are not so weakened as you assume; they are shifting, is all. It feels to many now that their cognitive functions are not what they were. And yet, this is only a sign of the Ascension journey. It is similar to other physical symptoms that billions are experiencing, not a sign of degradation.

We understand that you do not wish to be immobilized in any way. Yet the greatest movement you carved out for yourself to experience in this Earth life was not physical but etheric. And so meditating, listening to high vibrational music, and speaking with your Spirit team, in addition to any positive and encouraging reading you are able to do, are your main occupations now, as you receive the cellular and etheric shifts that this immobility is assisting you in receiving.

Many have no idea that they have planned into their life charts a time of incapacity, whether through injury, illness, or disorder, because the etheric work they are doing, including soul growth, requires a physically quiet body, or even a nonmoving one.

Though this sounds cruel, strange, and almost unthinkable, it is so, and has been so for thousands of years. Your Spirit team can explain it more clearly, so ask them. They can easily download you with their wisdom, if you cannot hear them inwardly, so that the answers flow easily into your conscious mind in quiet moments.

The reasons are there. If you wish to speed up and accelerate your learning time and return to full mobility, or to experience a Peace-filled acceptance of where you are now, you can revise your life chart to reflect such.

Keep in mind that if your higher self feels that complete healing would interfere with the soul growth and Earth mission you came in with, they might possibly hold off that change for a while, to protect your original vision for this life.

## Be willing to allow the feelings of grief to come forth—feel them, but then release them and move on.

The feelings of grief over what you feel to have lost physically and musically are part of your adjustment to this new form of living. There is always a letting go. Even the person who knows their partner or spouse was not good for them, and that they needed to leave that relationship, will experience a time of grieving after doing so.

For you to feel that what you have loved and lived for so long could be out of reach now is an even greater shock. Yet the music you have experienced is still within you, and still ready to be loved and listened to by you. That too is a form of participation, and a valid one.

Be willing to allow the feelings of grief to come forth—to cry or rage or ask "Why?" at times. Feel them, but then release them and move on.

Grief, anger, feelings of abandonment, and other dense emotions are not a pleasant thing to experience. Yet you grieve far more than your current situation. You grieve also for many lifetimes of loss.

In this, you gain understanding now that eluded you while you still had full mobility.

Your new life is at this time one of releasing the old life. Should mobility return, that old life will still be gone. Every day is a new start for everyone, regardless of the continuity that they believe occurs from one day to the next. That is an illusion. Those on a path of Light awaken every morning a new and different being (a higher vibrational one) than they were the day before.

This signals the kind of Transformation that will make more sense to you as time moves on. Even if you are only able to retain a small amount of movement (including your thinking ability), you are able to live more fully than you now imagine. In fact, imagination will become one of your closest allies in understanding this new world you find yourself in.

For you have moved to a timeline of higher thought, higher vibrational forms of experience, and encounters with higher beings who, though you may not be aware of them in your awake time, are guiding you through this time of Transformation and Transfiguration.

You are still fully committed to and accomplishing your Earth life mission, and your soul mission.

And so yes, release the grief as needed, then give yourself some positive work to do.

Visualize the children in the world (or the elderly, the homeless, those caught in war zones, or some other population in need of support), by inwardly imaging one child in need of Love and support. Step into their situation, and put a hand on their shoulder, or pick them up and hold them, assuring them that all is well. That they are not alone. And that their cries for help do not go unheard.

Be their advocate, their companion, their reassurance. Image a ray of Light going from your heart to theirs—knowing that as you do so, all in their situation are receiving that Light on a higher level, that will flow down into their daily life and awareness.

You are an Ambassador of Light, and not one confined to a solid place of immobility at all, but open to the experiences of the higher realms. You are on a journey to lift the spirits of humankind, whatever their struggles and pains.

While your frustration is with having lack of movement for the moment, your gratitude is in realizing that nothing can put a cap on your spirit, even if it appears that you are in a helpless state outwardly. You are anything but.

Understand that the soul remains powerful, even when mind, body, and emotions appear spent or held back in some way. Know that you are not alone, and that as you travel etherically in your spirit body each night, you are a part of the music of the spheres, adding your own tonal vibration to its perfect Oneness and place of completion.

You have not been abandoned, though your path is a demanding and challenging one. If you can compare yourself more to the mountain climber or cliff climber who is taking on a challenge that many warn against, that is far closer to the form of journey you are on. Characterizing yourself as helpless and immobile does not accurately describe your experience, though you may feel that at times.

## All who consciously journey a dark and difficult path, seeking Divine Love and higher wisdom, leave a powerful Light in their wake.

And things will not always be thus. You will be shown the path in ways that offer Light to you, body and soul, in ways that

Light up your inner self to shine in its brightest way, despite how others or even your own ego-mind may assume you are doing.

Accept this journey and bless it, even praise and thank it, each day. Let it know you are ready to release it and to return to full health if that is for your higher good, and that you are accepting only that which is for your higher good now.

All who consciously journey a dark and difficult path, seeking Divine Love and higher wisdom, leave a powerful Light in their wake that shifts the entire environment of that path to a higher level, a higher experience for everyone coming after them.

If you are able to learn about energy healing, or are already trained in such, you may wish to spend your day extending that as well as comfort to every person, population, and part of the Earth in need of such, as well as to your own body and spirit.

Establish these vibrations of serving, giving, and receiving higher Light throughout your day, and they will become your natural frequency, beaming out from you in brilliant power, whether you are fully mobile or not, in high or low spirits, waking or sleeping.

Far from there being less for you to do now, there is more. And the music, brilliant thought, and leaps and bounds of your soul will find its way to expressing that, dear one. Now and in all ways.

We are with you, all of us here in the higher realms, each with our own path to tread, and yet each part of the great Divinely lit whole.

We are with you! You are never alone.

# 19

# On Making Wise Choices and Trusting Intuitive Guidance

*I feel that the Universe just toys with me; I do the right thing at the wrong time, and the wrong thing at the right time, again and again, throughout my whole life.*

*Even though I do lots of research and deep soul searching, and something feels RIGHT in the gut, later I realize that I followed the wrong cues, and again made the wrong decision.*

*How do I get myself on track, with a sense of real purpose and joy and happiness in life, and hope for the future? (All of which I don't feel now.)*

W e would say, that it is not so much a matter of your not doing the right thing at the right time, so much as allowing yourself to express from the high heart, and then not judging your actions or decisions based on apparent outcomes.

You are not always mistaken, in all of these situations you refer to. At times a sharp turn is taken and an unexpected outcome occurs because that is the way in which you have, on a higher level, chosen to learn of your own higher instincts and intuition. You are capable of loving yourself enough that you don't automatically criticize yourself or feel to have done the wrong thing, based on what you see before you.

Even a person who engages in soul searching and researches the issue fully, as you say, is still capable of walking down a path that turns out to be more demanding, not less. Sometimes there is more learned in the times when you are stretched, feel to be have done or said the wrong thing, or feel to have been left behind by your own wise counsel. In these moments, you learn more of who you are, and what needs to be healed, restored, or released. You also begin to realize how vital it is to extend Love to yourself in all situations.

It appears that there are energetic influences at work that are putting you off a path of greater ease and comfort, and though you can most assuredly learn from that, constant frustration in life is not a positive path.

You also hold the subconscious belief that, "No matter which way I turn, I end up at the wrong destination." We would begin immediately revising that belief into one that is vibrationally higher and more positive, and that allows you to move forward with decisions, without feeling "I'll no doubt make a mistake this time, as I have other times."

Most assuredly, the Universe is not toying with you. That is not how the Universe works. There is no higher purpose in laughing at someone's struggle or intentionally leading them astray. As we say, there are influences at work of a much lower order that are throwing off your inner compass and causing you to doubt yourself.

You are also at times judging some outcomes as negative—and on the surface, they may appear that way—which in fact are not as negative as you assume.

## We would write out affirmations such as, "I Am perfectly led by Divine Wisdom. I always choose what is for my and others' higher good."

We strongly recommend looking at whatever feels not to be working in your life, and working on those areas with affirmations, or other forms of retraining the subconscious to believe the positive and to work with you, not against you.

We would write out by hand, over and over, affirmations such as, "I Am perfectly led by Divine Wisdom in all my decisions. I always choose what is for my and others' higher good." Write this 25 times or more, every day, for at least a month.

Is this excessive? No! You are revising deep-seated beliefs and rerouting neural pathways in the brain that have filled you with self-doubt for years. Do not wait for some Universal force to swoop down and pull you out of what you have created to pull yourself out of, experiencing all the learning that comes with that.

As you write out your new reality over and over each day, it will become a part of your spirit, body, and mind. Your energies will link with this new energy, and accept it as your Truth. There is no reason to feel left behind regarding making wise decisions. Yet you must also come to where you can be at Peace with a decision, and not judge yourself harshly afterward.

Once you have made any decision, release it to the higher realms, and say to your higher self and to the Universe, "Divine Will be done! I am at Peace. I release this entire situation to Divine Wisdom and Divine Light."

Energy clearings from a capable shaman or energy healer are also very important—as we note elsewhere, there are a number of reputable practitioners online who clear people's energies of entities, energy forms, and family, cultural, and ancestral beliefs, presences, and traumas. Much is offered at low or no cost online, particularly recorded clearings, and should be taken advantage of. Research these and see what works best for you. One of the reasons you and so many others have come back to the Earth in this lifetime is to release that which is more fully and powerfully released while on the Earth than in the higher dimensions.

It is also a necessary part of coming into the fifth dimension, to release all that would not exist in that higher frequency. Otherwise, one moves far more slowly into those levels of understanding and spiritual adeptness that the fifth dimension naturally offers those who resonate with it.

Your sense of purpose, Joy, and happiness may well come from serving others. We do not mean, that you should quit whatever you are doing now in life and go off to some poverty-stricken area to help those who appear to be helpless.

You can serve others at every moment, offering Love and acceptance, a warm, kind and helpful presence, and belief in the value of each person's life, no matter what your current job is. There are endless ways to be a positive support to others, just as there are endless ways to be a positive support to your own life.

It is entirely up to you to locate what makes you most joyful, what gives you a sense of fulfillment that nothing else can, and what supports you and affirms *you* as the utterly unique and individual presence on the Earth that you are. There is no one like you, and that is by Divine design.

It is not necessary to make your financial income from the things that give you the most Joy, but it is vital to find them and live them out, on some level that is meaningful to you. This does not come from always "making the right decisions" and feeling that you are coloring inside the lines in life. It often comes from breaking rules—for example, releasing family or cultural expectations that you perform a certain job, marry a certain kind of person, or live a particular lifestyle—when those things are not true to your authentic self.

You will know when something rings true with your authentic self, because you will have a feeling of Lightness about it. You will know intuitively when something feels right, despite what others might say, and even despite initial outer results. Of course you want to remain respectful and kind toward yourself, others, the environment, etc. But within the basic parameters of showing Love and compassion to others, and respecting their boundaries, you are at a crossroads now, where you are asking yourself to step forward to find what makes you joyful, what makes you happy, what gives you a sense of purpose.

This is one of the most important journeys any human being can take. This is why we cannot prescribe for you what it is you should do, think, or be in order to arrive at that destination.

You are already on that road. And trusting yourself to do what is for your and others' higher good is a vital part of that journey, whatever the choice to be made at any one time.

It is also vital to notice those decisions you make, however small, that turn out well. So you might say to yourself, for example, "I had a great salad at lunchtime today. I always make the perfect food choices!" Or "These are great socks that I'm wearing. I always make the right choices, no matter what I buy." Or "There are so many advantages to where I live: [then name three of them]. I've chosen a wonderful place to live in, and the next one will be even better."

These may sound like strange things to say to yourself, because the ego-mind (and the subconscious) will assure you that saying these things means you are not being humble enough. That they are misplaced praises, and that to improve at anything, you must criticize yourself constantly. That's the only way to self-improvement, they will tell you.

And you must answer, "Self-Love is so powerful, and so transforming, that it is lifting me to a higher vibration at every moment." We can assure you that until you stop these inner criticisms of your decisions, actions, and lack of fulfillment, you will continue to experience more dissatisfaction.

This is why we strongly recommend writing out affirmations, and doing Emotional Freedom Technique (known as tapping). There is much information about the EFT method available in books, videos, and online. We also strongly recommend guided meditations that assist you in healing the child self, and in building up a stronger sense of self that is not based on judgment, but Love and acceptance.

Even just a few steps in the right direction will make a difference in your inner life, opening the way for you to start experiencing a kinder and more supportive inner self, who is ready to offer the wisdom of your higher self, spirit guides, and

Angelic guardians. This will assist you far more than a criticism that says, "You always do the wrong thing."

We encourage everyone to speak with their Spirit team each day. Ask them, "What do I need to know? Share your wisdom with me, friends!" Or ask about a particular situation that is troubling you, which you need higher insights on. They are more than happy to assist, as are all of us in the Collective, or any higher guide you wish to call on.

Ask, and open to receive. Say, "If I do not hear you inwardly, send me the energy of your wisdom into my heartspace. I know it will come up in my conscious mind in perfect time and way."

Sometimes your Spirit team will speak to you through outer messages—something you read or overhear, or something that someone mentions in casual conversation. Messages can come in a song or a slogan. Or via a symbol that suddenly seems powerful and relevant, even if you do not understand why at first.

### Walk with your Spirit team and the Universe by giving over to them all outcomes, giving thanks at all times for perfect results and perfect processes.

All of these are vital moments. All of them are messages that answer what you are asking to understand. There is no reason to feel the futility of your actions or that your questions are not being heard and answered.

Another important factor to making wise decisions that serve the higher good of you and all involved, is working from the heartspace, rather than simple researching the information available, and expecting that that information will be sufficient.

It will never be sufficient. Outer information does not take into account the wisdom and heart-based intuitive understanding of your higher self, who is able to look out over your life and view it as a whole, including your future.

Your higher self is always able to see how decisions will impact you and others over time. This is one of the reasons that we ask that you do not automatically judge a decision as "bad" based purely on what seems to have occurred. You do not know what any outer situation will ultimately bring to your or another's path, and what it may reveal to you or another over time.

Before you make any decision, of course you will wish to look into the specifics of the situation. Then before acting, speak with your higher self and guides. Ask for their input and guidance, which is vital to making wise decisions that take into account future probabilities as well as your higher good. Some people find muscle testing to be helpful in locating a clear Yes or No answer to a question.

Once you have meditated and required a higher answer, place the entire situation in the hands of this loving Universe, and your kind, supportive Spirit team. Request and require that they ensure that only that which is for the higher good of all take place now.

At that point, you have done your work. Let go, and let life flow, while sending Light to that process that all will support everyone involved in higher ways. Realize too, that others' intentions, expectations, and will are also involved in every circumstance. You do not operate independent of others' intentions.

And so release that which does not belong to you energetically, and walk with your Spirit team and the Universe by giving over to them all outcomes, and giving thanks at all times for perfect results and perfect processes that lead you further every day into the Joy and fulfillment you seek.

It is a great part of your path to increasingly come to love and accept yourself as a sacred Light Being who is only here to do good, to love and serve all, and to know the Joy of your life journey.

You have not been abandoned, and you are not being toyed with. You are being shown a higher path.

# 20

# On Calling Upon the Higher Realms for Help

*Daily I am assaulted by the cruelty of humanity. Children caged, pollution, injustice, extrajudicial killings. It does not seem to get better; it seems to get worse. You could say that the news just makes it seem worse, but get real.*

*Mass shootings are a new phenomenon. Bribery [of public officials] is at its highest level ever, and totally blatant. More pollution than ever.*

*Some who channel hold Trump in the highest esteem, despite his obvious violent crimes and cruelty. The public relations influences, both for and against him and Hillary, seem unending.*

*We are told by many that he is waging a war against evil, as if he were a god.*

*To me, it seems like a lot of brainwashing. And yet, it goes on. Especially within the spiritual community, where some see him as Saint Germain.*

*Many young people do not believe this nonsense, and can see what it obviously is: totally nuts. Many older ones just seem to try to buy into this. (Though this doesn't apply in every case.)*

*We have been told by one channeler that Trump is taking us to a higher plane, protecting us, fighting a terrible cabal.*

*All I see him doing in the physical universe is stepping up the destruction created from pollution. If he's so great, why does he hate Nature? Animals? The ecosystem? How can he be Saint Germain, if he doesn't even follow the United States constitution?*

*Either way, while the two sides argue, our planet is being destroyed by pollution. I don't think we can wait much longer for help. We need help now.*

*We are enslaved, so long as we can't even figure out what is true. It's obvious things are getting much worse, not better, as far as our destroying the ecosystem.*

*If we ask for help, can you please help us wake up? We need to be freed. We are enchained. Help us, please.*

*What can we do to get more help for our Mother Gaia?*

We are utterly aware of Earth's current status, both as you describe it and as we ourselves view it, though there are real differences in those two viewpoints. We also fully understand your feeling that you have only so much time to work things out, before irreparable damage is done to Lady Gaia.

Regarding our sending help to Earth and Her people, we have in fact been assisting Earth for many thousands of years—as Galactic family members, as higher dimensional nonphysical entities, as energy forms and intentions, and as other etheric forms.

Though Earth is a free will planet, you have never been abandoned, nor will you be.

Catastrophes in one form or another have been averted numerous times, and will continue to be, as needed. This includes the slower effects of toxic radiation and other forms of pollution in air, water, soil, crops, and other areas of Earth's body, as well as our stopping nuclear warheads from deploying, or rerouting those that have been deployed and overseeing their controlled detonation well out into space, where they will harm no one.

Were we not already assisting Earth and Her animals, plant life, and humanity, you would by now have succumbed to the malaise you describe.

## Your free will is a thing to be fully respected and honored by us, and by all in this Universe.

We understand your concern and unhappiness at all that the Earth and her people are suffering. Yet understand that your free will on this planet has already been usurped, by invaders who came thousands of years ago to occupy and rule your planet in unjust and highly imbalanced ways.

We would be only a bit higher in our intentions, if we suddenly "flew down and rescued humanity" as they say. You would then view *us* as your overlords, and look to us for solutions and even permission to live your lives and run your communities in certain ways. This would not be an improvement—you have seen how some spiritual teachers believe themselves to be following a higher path, and then, once they have amassed a following, fall into ego and express a far lower intention than they began with.

Your free will is a thing to be fully respected and honored by us, and by all in this Universe. And your innate power—your sovereignty, your growing consciousness, and your ability to save yourselves—is a thing for you all to become fully aware of, to grab by the horns, and to fully enact. We cannot do this *for* you—that would defeat the entire purpose behind your Ascension! Nor would we attempt to do so.

You speak of Awakening, and we wish to say that we are seeing at this time an Awakening on your planet such as only dreamt of by earlier generations of poets, sages, and spiritual seekers. We cannot agree that most in the spiritual community, as you term it, are followers of dark entities (and false life forms) posing as human beings. Nor can we agree that all young people have caught on to what certain political figures are intending. The landscape of awareness is colorful and varied.

Understand that you live in a world in which human beings have long been subject to numerous forms of humiliation, degradation, overt mind control, subtle mental programming, and a mass desperation created from carefully designed economic and political situations, including political revolutions that only reinstated the elite in a slightly different way.

Understandably, you may now have a hard time believing that all of these lies, illusions, and hypnosis could ever allow even one independent human thought.

## As you have now entered the Sat Yuga—a time of Enlightenment, Peace, Prosperity, and Justice— we do not see Earth as headed for disaster.

And indeed, they are not "allowing" that. The independent thought—the Awakening—we see happening now has nothing to do with the old way of experiencing life on Earth. You have asked no one's permission for it. It has everything to do with growing a consciousness sprung from the soul level, from experiencing and aspiring to the reality enjoyed in the higher realms. And from the co-Creative essence of your own spirits, as they reach higher in the empowering energies now coming to Earth.

If it were any other era, such as the era before the one you have just entered—the Kali Yuga, which was an era of destruction—we might agree with you that Earth consciousness was generally low. But as you have now entered the Sat Yuga—a time of Enlightenment, Peace, Prosperity, and Justice—we do not see Earth as headed for disaster in a short amount of time, and that She and all of you require rescuing.

All of what you name—the cruelty, violence, corruption—is coming into the Light now, and being shown for what it truly is: a violation of human spirit, human sovereignty, and Divine Law. Those at the head of these schemes are even now, in some cases, facing courts of Divine Justice, on Earth and on other planets. They are not escaping simply by jumping into underground hideouts or leaping aboard a spacecraft. We are aware of where they are, and when and how they are being brought to face their crimes and answer for them.

Some of the shadow realm are coming into the Light now— by their own free will, and that is as it should be. The idea of forcing situations or people has had its day, and will not be permitted to continue.

Now, did we decide all of that? No—all of *you* did. Planet Earth, and the majority of Her people, on a higher level and now increasingly on an Earthly level. And that too is as it should be.

## Hold a concentration of Love and higher Light for Earth and all Her beings each day.

And so, we would say, watch or read very little of news reports and channeled material that do not give you a fuller picture, that your inner being does not resonate with in peaceful ways. (And you are correct that there is no politician who embodies the spirit of St Germain now. St Germain is himself still incarnate upon the Earth, as he has been for centuries, and working on behalf of the presence and power of higher Light on the planet.)

The news media report the dense and the painful because a negative slant on your world is how the now defunct old regime kept your consciousness low, and expecting disaster at any moment. Fear and desperation were always their most useful forms of enslavement. But those days have been ending for a while now, and will continue to fade.

There are independent news reports that seek actual Truth, in the sense of establishing what Justice really is, and what it means to humankind, and how it may be established as the norm, not the exception. Yet we would caution you to not take in too much of even those reports.

These are by and large situations over which you have no immediate control. Yet you have powerful influence. Hold a concentration of Love and higher Light for Earth and all Her beings each day, giving thanks for the freedom and sovereignty of both planet and living beings.

That is by far a million times more positive, healing, and life-building than watching the news or discussing it with someone, and feeling your energy sink lower as a result. Consider that you are, with your Light Being presence on the Earth right now, a healer of the highest order, and that you must keep your thoughts on a high frequency so as to anchor and activate more fully that which you came here to embody—the Light that heals, frees, and celebrates humanity at every moment.

We celebrate your sensitivity, your insight, and the beauty of your very deep compassion. We would merely say, "Allow yourself any Joy you can possibly find. Go look for it, and celebrate all that you can, giving thanks throughout the day."

That experience, transmitted through the ethers, will elevate your planet and humanity in ways that we of the higher realms could once have only dreamt of for your beautiful Earth.

# 21

# On Finishing Your Ascension and Life Mission "on Time"

*I had to step away from practicing my healing art, because I have to concentrate on healing myself first.*

*I have so many personal issues coming up now to be understood and cleansed, that I feel I might be left behind if I don't hurry up, yet I know healing can't be rushed.*

*Do I have time to work it all out and Ascend? And how will I know when my work is complete, if it ever can be here on Earth?*

Your initial comment is one of the most relevant issues for any energy worker to consider at this time. And it is not surprising that so many are thinking of it, in this era of profound change and renewal.

There is a degree to which healing yourself is intimately tied in to the work of healing others, though you and other facilitators of healing (for in truth, all healing is actually self-healing) may not always be aware of such. We would say, if you feel steady enough to work at least one or two days a week, with one person a day, then you may well have positive contributions to make to the lives of others, even as you move forward with transforming your own challenges.

All have personal issues arising now. These issues are demanding to be heard, understood, and cleansed so that your spirit and psyche are free of them. Yet there is no need to rush or feel hurried in any way.

You are right, when you say that healing cannot be rushed. That one idea in and of itself should indicate to you that you are moving into profound renewal and upward Ascension, and that Time is increasingly irrelevant on that path.

You are in fact stepping out of Time, along with everyone and everything else on the Earth that is Ascending. And so that old third dimensional paradigm of, "Will I have enough time?" becomes increasingly irrelevant, because you are no longer dealing with life from that viewpoint. Even if your mind is somewhat stuck in the old paradigm, and presents such to you often, your spirit is not stuck in it.

For those on the Ascension path, Time is not an issue. You move forward at the pace and in the way that is right for you, for your unique journey. You will of course Ascend, whether you do so in a body or out of it. And you are of course here to assist others in their journey.

Your life of service to others is a part of your path, not something that runs parallel to your path, or in opposition to it. That work is also never fully complete, nor need it be.

**It is not a question of "doing it all" or "getting it done," but of simply Being in all your beauty and glory, appreciating the only moment that exists— the Present One.**

Again—the linear notion of Beginning, Forward Movement, and End are third dimensional in nature. No one in the higher realms stresses over whether there is enough Time to finish any effort or point of focus. All unfolds in perfect time and way upon the Earth as well, because all in this Universe is in a constant state of Becoming. Everything occurring in the higher realms also presents itself in the context of the Now moment. Creation can occur with a word or a thought.

In essence, your Ascension path and your life of service are no different. It is a construct of the ego-mind to yelp nervously, "We might not have enough *time* to do it all—to finish what we came here to do!"

How could you possibly finish? How does Love decide one day that it has done enough, and then sit down, sigh, and look around for something else to do?

You are Love Itself, in human form. It is not a question of "doing it all" or "getting it done," but of simply Being in all your beauty and glory, while appreciating the only moment that exists—the Present One.

This is why one of your finest, most enlightened teachers, Eckart Tolle, has written that "there has never been a time in your life that has not been Now, and there never will be." He is pointing to a higher reality than the clock on the wall or the calendar. He is pointing to the path of higher service and of all existence that continues on, without timeline, without reference to Beginning or End.

Your Earth mission is far more than what you are "doing" at any one time. In a sense, it began before you incarnated, and has always been in place, and always will be, expressing itself in myriad ways over different incarnations, higher intentions, and forms, on the Earth and elsewhere in the Universe.

## You are experimenting inside the paradigm of finite measures of Time, but you are not trapped by them.

And so we would say, release yourself from the need to see an end to the horizon (you would be disappointed to see one!), and allow yourself the beautiful empowerment of knowing that Love does not end, and neither does your path of growth. Let yourself realize that you are ever-expanding, and that whether that takes place here, or you decide to continue it in a higher dimension, you are still contributing magnificently now, purely by being here upon the Earth at this moment.

You are experimenting inside the paradigm of finite measures of Time, but you are not trapped by them, nor is any part of your life defined by them, on a soul level. It is only the Earth consciousness that nervously decides "we may not have time to finish," and measures things purely in terms of "things I got done today."

Begin now to free yourself of this incessant rush and pressure to get things done by a certain day and time. Understand that whenever and however you are able to assist others—and you are anchoring higher energies into the Earth and human consciousness, purely by being here—that time and way is perfect and holds its own expression of Divinity.

No, you can never get it all done! And that means that the joy of Discovery, the Great Adventure that is life in this Universe— that road goes ever on and on, "down from the door where it began" to quote our friend Tolkien again. ("And whither then? I cannot say.")

And you would not have had it any other way.

# Resources

**Books**

*Manifesting 1, 2, 3* by Ken Elliott

*The Power of Now* and *The New Earth* by Eckhart Tolle

*The Empath's Survival Guide: Life Strategies for Sensitive People* by Judith Orloff

**Energy Work**

Channeling sessions with the Collective - https://carolineoceana ryan.com/channeled-readings-ask-the-collective/

Energy and Entity Clearings by Bonnie Serratore - https://www .spiritualacceleration.com/group-clearings/

Energy and Entity Clearings by Dave Barnett - http://davethe mystic.com

Bio-Energy Detection, Re-Balancing, and Healing - Dr Vinayak - http://electrumhealth.com

Emotional Freedom Technique (Tapping) - https://www.the tappingsolution.com

High Vibrational Music – YouTube search - https://www.you tube.com/results?search_query=high+vibrational+music+

[These links accessible as of December 2018]

# About the Author

Caroline Oceana Ryan is an author, channeler, speaker, and radio host of *The Empowered Lightworker* on LNMRadioNetwork.com. She has channeled information from Angels and spirit guides since childhood.

She currently channels the wisdom and higher energies of the Collective, a group that includes the Ascended Masters, Angels and Archangels, Galactic beings, the Faery elders, Earth elementals, and other higher beings assisting humanity in Ascending to the fifth dimension.

*Earth Life Challenges* is the third book in the Fifth Dimensional Life series, which includes *Abundance For All: The Lightworker's Way to Creating Money and True Wealth* and *Connections: The Collective Speak on Romance and Friendship*. Other popular books by the Collective include *The Ascension Manual* – Parts One and Two.

Ryan holds an MA in intercultural education and theology from the Union Theological Seminary in New York City. In 2014 she published the travel memoir *Adventures in Belfast: Northern Irish Life After the Peace Agreement*. All books are available on Amazon.

She has published poetry in the United States, England, and Ireland. Her plays *A Witch's Cross* and *Rage Removers* were produced at the Sunset Gardner Stages in West Hollywood.

Visit www.CarolineOceanaRyan.com to sign up for the weekly "Message to Lightworkers" channelings, and for information on channelings sessions, live interviews and events, the Abundance Group, and guided meditations by the Collective.

# Other Books Channeled from the Collective

## Also from the Fifth Dimensional Life series:

*Abundance For All: The Lightworker's Way to Creating Money and True Wealth* (2016)

*Connections: The Collective Speak on Romance and Friendship* (2017)

## The Ascension Manual series:

*The Ascension Manual – Part One: A Lightworker's Guide to Fifth Dimensional Living* (2015)

*The Ascension Manual – Part Two: Creating a Fifth Dimensional Life* (2016)

## Also by Caroline Oceana Ryan

*Adventures in Belfast: Northern Irish Life After the Peace Agreement* (2014)

**Available on Amazon**

Made in the USA
San Bernardino, CA
21 December 2018